Chet
The Missing Years

A Memoir

By

Artt Frank

Praise for Chet Baker: The Missing Years, A Memoir by Artt Frank

In August of 2012, jazz great Dave Brubeck gave the following review of Artt's memoir:

"Artt Frank, the author of **Chet Baker: The Missing Years** *is a devout Christian who practices what he preaches. His personal memoir of his meeting and subsequent friendship with the jazz genius of the trumpet is an unvarnished, honest portrayal of Chet Baker. In depicting Chet's struggle to recovery, Artt reveals great compassion for a sensitive soul fighting for a life, and puts to rest the rumors and gossip that circulated about Chet's 'missing years.'"*

– **Dave Brubeck,** Legendary Jazz Pianist and Composer

"A natural storyteller in the oral tradition, Artt's gifts at dialog and narrative shine in this new book, except here the tale is true, and the material is from Artt's exciting and heart-rending years with his jazz brother, Chet Baker. Artt knew Baker's jazz life. He lived it with him, on and off the bandstand ... This book is a jazz history gift and a long-lost narrative prayer."

– **Kevin Rabas,** Professor, Drummer, and Author of *Bird's Horn* and *Sonny Kenner's Red Guitar*

"**Chet Baker: The Missing Years** *is perhaps the most accurate account of Chet's life and true spirit to date. Superbly written by Artt Frank ... the book gives fresh insight into the man behind the music. A must-read for everyone from the casual jazz fan to the serious student of jazz history."*

– **JB Dyas**, PhD, VP, Education and Curriculum Development, Thelonious Monk Institute of Jazz

"As Chet Baker's Boswell, Artt Frank provides great insight into the life and music of an overlooked, tragic genius in jazz. A must read for fans of Chet Baker and jazz."

– **Chuck Haddix**, Author of *Bird: The Life and Music of Charlie Parker* and *Kansas City Jazz: From Ragtime to Bebop--A History*

"**Chet Baker: The Missing Years** *takes the reader back to a time and a place where jazz musicians, movie stars and rock stars rubbed shoulders in smoke-filled clubs along Sunset Boulevard, and where a fallen angel could rise up out of the street, and with the love of his loyal friend, dust off his wings, and learn to fly again."*

– Tim Schaffner, Publisher and Drummer

Artt Frank,
Oklahoma Jazz Hall of Fame Bop Drummer

"Artt is one of those unsung heroes of the Be Bop era...He can be firm with the sticks and subtle with the brushes, but also subtle with sticks and firm with brushes; he can swing without making a lot of noise, without raising his voice. All this made him the drummer Chet Baker loved to work with when he started his comeback around 1969."

– **Jeroen de Valk,** Author of *Chet Baker: His Life and Music*

"You go upstairs, you go downstairs... No matter where you go musically, Artt's playing is always in the pocket!"

– **Al Cohn**, Legendary Tenor Saxophonist

"If anyone has inherited Chet's musical soul, I would say it is Artt Frank."

– **Ali Ryerson**, Jazz Flutist for Billy Taylor, Kenny Barron, Stephane Grappelli, Art Farmer, Joe Beck

"Artt Frank doesn't just play drums: he plays music!"

– **Stan Levey**, Jazz Drumming Great with Dizzy Gillespie, Charlie Parker, Ella Fitzgerald, Miles Davis...

"Artt is the drummer's drummer. Give Artt a pair of brushes or sticks and he'll make a garbage can cover sound like the most expensive snare drum. This cat swings."

– **Teddy Kotick**, Former Bassist with Charlie Parker, Horace Silver and Bill Evans, and two years with Artt Frank's Quintet

"Artt is the real shit, man. His groove is so rooted!"

– **Phil Markowitz**, Jazz Pianist

Chet Baker: The Missing Years

A Memoir

By

Artt Frank

Chet Baker: The Missing Years
A Memoir by Artt Frank

Published by BooksEndependent, LLC
www.BooksEndependent.com

Cover photo by Tim Schaffner, by permission
Cover and Book Design by J.D. Woods Consulting

Publisher's Note:

This memoir is about Artt Frank and his fond memories of his friendship and musical collaborations with the jazz icon, Chet Baker. This is an independent work, and is not sponsored or endorsed by or otherwise affiliated with the estate of Chet Baker.

ISBN: 978-0-9887687-4-1

Also by Artt Frank

Essentials for the Be Bop Drummer
with Pete Swan,
Schaffner Press, Inc., 2004

Dedication

First, I want to give complete and total honor, glory, praise and thanksgiving to the one true Almighty God and to my Lord and Savior, Yeshua, for the gifts of life, and the innate ability to play and compose beautiful music.

I dedicate this book to the memory of my dearest mother and father, Rose and Clayton H. Frank; to my four departed siblings, Bernard, Donald, Teddy and Pauline; and to my beloved remaining sisters, Barbara Webb and Brenda Duncan.

To my precious wife and soul mate, Lisa, without whom, I wouldn't be here today, and that's a fact. She's my world. She is my everything!!!

To my closest friend, Chet Baker, he shall forever be a major part of my life.

Table of Contents

Foreword

This is a book of Artt Frank's memoirs of time spent with the legendary jazz trumpet player Chet Baker. I would guess Chet has in some way influenced a great majority of all trumpeters, past and present... and hopefully, in the future as well.

What a great honor that Artt has asked me to write something as a foreword to his new book about the great Chet Baker. After recovering from the shock that went with this honored request, I thought how easy this would be for me because of my life-long reverence for Chet's playing. Then, after getting into the book, I realized this was not just another ordinary book in the style of a documentary on Chet's life. It read much more like a script to a movie, as it was highly conversational and almost "visual." Throughout the book, I oftentimes felt like a "fly on the wall" or an eavesdropper, privately being allowed on the inside of Artt's personal relationship with Chet, both on the bandstand and off.

Artt's ability to re-create situations of his constant adventures, musically and socially, is phenomenal. He refers to the many notes he kept, somewhat like a diary, and these allow him to re-create conversations they had about the music, Chet's family, friends, love affairs, and problems with his survival as a person.

Mark Twain stated, "A lie can travel halfway around the world while the truth is putting on its shoes!" My collection of books on Chet Baker's life contains more contradictions than I can recall. Stories I have been told by players I met and who had played with or known Chet personally do not always tell the truth... perhaps only that one person's opinionated truth. Separating fact from opinion has always been a major difficulty in life in general. I recall the conflicts in stories about Charlie Parker, the accent always being stressed upon his drug problems rather than his positive qualities as a person and as a great creative artist. It seems Chet has also been unfairly and improperly served.

One thing that struck me many times throughout the reading of this book was that I kept thinking, "Wouldn't it be nice if everyone knew these inside things about Chet?" I kept finding out little things that were in his mind about his family, his playing, his ideas, his influences, and of course, his problems and how he chose to deal with them. Artt's conversations with Chet allow many insights that I had never been aware of in previous publications about him. For example... his love of apple pie and vanilla ice cream! But wait; am I giving away too much info here? You have to READ about it all! That's the real thing.

This is a book about the respect, friendship, and very deep love Artt Frank had, and of course, STILL has, for his mentor, his bandstand brother, his musical guide in many ways. How fortunate that he had the opportunity to spend the better part of his life with Chet Baker and how fortunate for us that he has made this great effort to share that life with us... from the INSIDE!!!

Bobby Shew, Legendary Jazz Band Leader, Trumpet and Flugelhorn Musician/Composer/Professor

Preface

"It seemed to me that Chet was so focused on music and playing, that he spent most of his life with his eyes closed. Yet, he always seemed to know what was happening."

A.F.

This memoir is the heartfelt story of how I remember Chet Baker – the man, his music, and our long and memorable friendship. It is a poignant story of one man's struggle with drug addiction, pain, agony and sorrow. A brutal beating at the hands of five hoodlums left this lyrical trumpeter with the loss of four upper front teeth, and permanent trigeminal nerve damage to his face and jaw. Three medical doctors and a neurologist informed Chet that the possibility of his playing trumpet again was, at most, a strong improbability.

This is the story of how this musician, with the help, compassion and understanding of his loving wife, and the friendship of which I was honored to share, overcame near impossible odds and, over a period of agonizing months of struggle, learned how to play trumpet all over again. He continued to mature, and in so doing, developed a style and tone so distinctive that it set him apart from all other trumpet players.

The profound statement once coined by bop/jazz immortal Charlie "Bird" Parker, "*Ain't no way you can play it unless you lived it!*" was painfully brought to life by Chet Baker. I know of only a handful of musicians in the history of jazz of whom it can truthfully be said, "*the man lived to play and played to live.*"

There have been many negative and malicious things said about Chet after his death, both verbal as well as in print, by those who actually never knew the length, breadth, width or depth of this quiet, introspective genius. Chet isn't around to respond to those people, but I am!

For all that's been said and written about him in the negative vein, I was blessed to have known another side of the man; for example, the compassionate way he treated street people, the downtrodden and less fortunate. The critics and writers either didn't care, or didn't want to take the time to look deeper into the heart of the man who played so lyrically. Instead, they seemed intent to focus on the man's physical weaknesses rather than the true beauty coming from within. Therein lies the greater loss and error because they either could not, or willingly chose not, to hear the God-given beauty emanating from his voice or whatever brand of trumpet or flugelhorn Chet chose to play at any given performance.

For anyone out there who may still believe that Chet copied Miles Davis, please allow me to set the record straight once and for all time. Miles was a trained musician who studied musical theory at the famed Julliard School of Music. Chet, on the other hand was a complete and totally God-gifted jazz musician who played 100 percent by ear; who in my personal estimation, was the most hauntingly melodic, swinging player of all time, including all and barring none!

What I write about in this book is completely unfiltered – straight from the source. I reveal a side of Chet the world knew nothing about. I do this through my own direct observations of him, personal notes, and through Chet's own words. As a drummer, I am also a complete and total 'ear player' without formal training of any kind. This causes me to rely solely on my ears, and my ears are always attuned to everything around me. Listening is pretty much the way I take in the world. This was especially true in the many conversations I had with Chet over the years.

In music, particularly in jazz, being an ear player means you must be able to hear and learn a tune you've never heard before, then play it note-for-note whenever the leader calls for it to be played. And each time, you also need to remember the form, the feel, and the time the tune is set in. The more you play the tune, the more acquainted your mind and ears become with it until it becomes second nature. That's how it was between Chet and me, both on and off the stand. This is why each time I think of him, I can remember quite vividly the places we were, the time of day, and pretty much every word that was spoken.

So, to the best of my recollection, this is the way I remember Chet. Anyone looking for innuendo, sensationalism, fabrication, hearsay, lies, fantasy, or myth, will not find it in this book. You'll have to look elsewhere.

Readers will notice the name, Chet Baker, in the title of this book. Is it a biography of Chet? No. It is a book about my memories of the great times I had living a part of my life as a friend of, and playing jazz with, Chet Baker. The times I spent with him were absolutely well worth remembering and writing about. This is what I have done. That's all.

Artt Frank

Chapter 1
Our First Meeting

I met Chet Baker in March of 1954 in a Boston jazz club called, "Storyville." But the first time I *heard* Chet's music was over the Armed Forces radio aboard the USS Des Moines in '53 toward the end of the Korean War. Listening to Chet's trumpet on that radio, I cried inside, unable to understand how a trumpeter could affect a drummer so much. Right then, I sincerely sent up a prayer that I would get home safely and get a chance to meet and play with Chet Baker.

Since I was about six years old, I'd been playing drums on anything I could find. By the time I was in my teens, I tried to imitate the beats of my favorite drummer, Gene Krupa, on the tabletop at home in Westbrook, Maine. Still, the only other musician who had affected me the way Chet did, was when I first heard Charlie "Bird" Parker and the new form of jazz – Be Bop. At 17, I hitchhiked to New York City from Westbrook, just to hear Bird in person at The Royal Roost. And maybe get the courage to ask him if I could sit in. I did, and he and Max Roach were kind enough to let me play.

Now, at 21, the war was over, I was honorably discharged and home working at the paper mill, like my father and most everybody in Westbrook, and still in love with jazz and drumming.

Chet Baker had just won both the Downbeat and Metronome jazz magazine polls for America's number one new jazz trumpeter. That night in '54 when I got to Boston, the Storyville club was jam-packed. My first impression of him was not only was he gifted, but also he was a very handsome young man as evidenced by all the beautiful young girls surrounding him. I waited until most of the girls and fans left, then made my way over to the bandstand to say hello. I wanted to make him think we had met once before, so as I approached I extended my hand, and said, "Hi Chet, Art Frank. Remember me?"

He looked at me for what seemed an eternity, shook his head, and said, "No, no, I don't remember you, man. Sorry." He said it softly but directly. I learned right then and there that Chet was very quick, intent and painfully honest. He looked you in the eyes when he spoke. It seemed like he could pretty much read your thoughts on the spot. I got the feeling he'd tell you the truth even if it meant his losing a fan by doing so. Man, if Chet had been a gunfighter during the old Wild West days, he no doubt would have stared down Jesse James. That's how intense he was. And conversely, he was quite approachable.

As I spoke, he studied me for another few seconds or so and asked when and where we were supposed to have met. Rather than continuing to lie, I confessed that I hadn't really met him in person, but how terribly moved I'd been by his sound and the way he played when I'd first heard him on the radio aboard ship during the war. He smiled, obviously liking what I had said, and when he did, I couldn't help notice that one of his upper front teeth was missing on the left side. I was about to ask him how he'd lost it when the bass player, Carson Smith came over and stopped my train of thought. Chet introduced us, and we shook hands briefly. Carson excused himself and walked off toward the bar area. Chet didn't appear to be in any particular hurry to get rid of me, smiling and nodding at the beautiful young chicks as they walked by.

I went on to tell him about the prayer I'd made when I had first heard him play; that I'd be able to meet him one day, maybe even get the chance to play with him and his group. He studied me curiously and asked what instrument I played. I told him I was a drummer, and had sat in with Charlie Parker at the Royal Roost, and a lot of other great bop musicians along 52nd Street. Bop drummer Stan Levey had also given me a lot of inside tips on how to play. Chet seemed impressed and smiled warmly. As far as getting the chance to play with him one day, he said in his soft, melodic voice, "One never knows, man… one never knows."

Carson and Russ were on their way outside and asked Chet if he wanted to go out for a breath of fresh air. He nodded, excused himself and left me standing there. Much to my surprise though, he stopped, turned half way around and gestured for me to join him. I couldn't believe it. Here was Chet Baker inviting me to join him. Once outside the club, I lit up a cigarette and offered one to Chet. He just shook his head and told me he didn't smoke. He stood by watching the traffic whiz by. He had the interest and intensity of a little boy on some long ago Christmas morning watching his father operate a set of Lionel trains on a miniature set of tracks on a worn out linoleum covered floor.

After a minute or so, Russ and Carson told him they were going back inside the club, but Chet was too focused on watching all the cars go by and didn't respond. They left and I don't think Chet even realized I was standing there beside him until a minute or so later. He turned around and asked me where Russ and Carson had gone. When I told him what happened, his face lit up with a smile. He told me that whenever he watched a lot of cars speeding by, it brought to his mind one of the few things he would most like to do in life -- drive a race car at Le Mans and win. "What a thrill that would be, man," he said, a kind of daydream look in his eyes.

While I stood there listening to him, it occurred to me that I was talking to the nation's number one trumpet player, and he's telling me how he'd like to be a racecar driver. I told him he could probably do anything he set his mind to. Where I came from in Maine, racing cars against each other was what most of the young guys did every night and weekends for excitement. Hearing that brought another smile. He told me that most of the young cats in L.A. were doing the same thing. I guess it must have been pretty much the same way in every city and town across the country.

I asked him where he and his group were going after they left Boston. He said they would be doing back-to-back gigs in different cities before winding up doing a full month at "Birdland," the world-renowned jazz club in New York City. The first two weeks of that gig he would play opposite sets with Dizzy Gillespie's group, and the following two weeks, opposite sets with Miles Davis' group. He was real excited about the prospect of that. He was gracious and told me that if I could make it down during one of those weeks, I'd more than likely get the chance to sit in with him. I was ecstatic when he said that, and told him I'd do my damnedest to make it down on one of the nights he'd be sharing the stand with Miles Davis. He said he hoped so, and I believe he genuinely meant it.

I knew he had other things to do, and I didn't want to get off to a bad start by taking up any more of his time. He still had another set to play, and I had a hundred and five mile drive back to Westbrook, Maine. Also, I had to be at work at the paper mill by 6 a.m. the following morning. I worked the 'swing shift.' One week I'd work the 6 a.m. to 12 p.m. shift, the following week I'd work from 12 p.m. to 6 p.m., the next week I'd work from 6 p.m. to midnight, and finally, I'd work the graveyard shift, from midnight to 6 a.m. I hated the swing shift because it was very difficult to make plans to do anything. I really didn't want to leave the club, but knew I had to. I shook Chet's hand and told him I hoped to see him again when he played Birdland, and left the club reluctant, but elated.

Almost as soon as I had driven out of Boston, a mixture of snow and rain started to fall softly, causing the roads to be a bit slippery, not the least unusual in early spring. But I didn't care. I was absolutely ecstatic because I had finally met and talked with my main inspiration in jazz, Chet Baker, and he'd been very warm toward me. I praised and thanked God for hearing my prayers about meeting Chet.

The snow continued to fall but it never really amounted to anything, at least until I hit Route 1 in Maine, where the road became even more slippery. I made it home just before 5:00am, about the time my father would be getting up. He had to get up at that time each morning to get the wood stove fire going so he could make his 'Eight O'Clock' brand coffee. He'd have to do this in the spring, summer, fall and winter because we only had one wood-burning stove in the house and that was in the kitchen. Whenever I'd get home late, as I did in this case, I'd come upstairs very quietly so I wouldn't awaken him. But lo and behold, there he was, already up, dressed and sitting at the table waiting for the coffee to finish perking.

It seemed that every winter morning in Maine was a particularly cold one, and this March morning was no different. My father busied himself putting pieces of wood into the stove in order to have it warm for my mother and the other kids who'd soon be getting up. I swear, every other room in that apartment was freezing and the floors were as cold as glaciers. There was absolutely no insulation or storm windows, no central heating system nor even running hot water. In order to have hot water, we would have to fill a pan with water and heat it on the front of the stove.

This was a routine my father did each and every morning before he would sit down and enjoy his cup of coffee - after which, he'd put on his light weight frock coat, a railroad cap, leave the house and go out into the freezing cold. Not having a car, he'd walk the mile and a half through deep snow to get to work at the local paper mill. But God bless his heart, he was happy for me when I told him about the whole episode of meeting Chet. My dad played a C Melody sax, which is comparable to a soprano saxophone, but he never really got the opportunity to play in any of the nightclubs in nearby Portland. He was too busy working seven days of every week to support seven of us kids.

While we sat there talking, my mother woke up and joined us. Still being excited, I went over the whole story again, filling in each and every little detail, and later the same day, I relived it again with my three brothers and three sisters. I know it sounds crazy, but that's how important it was for me to have met Chet Baker.

My mother, having a 'steel trap' memory, recalled how I'd bought a record by Chet the year before, the day after my discharge, and wanted me to play it. I got the turntable from my room and played it for them. Hell, all I did for weeks and weeks was play *The Lamp is Low* on that Chet Baker record until I nearly wore the grooves out. There was something in Chet's music that got to me. I was so excited about the possibility of seeing Chet again that I wanted to share his music with everybody. I'd open the windows and play his record so the neighbors next door would be able to hear the sounds too. Some of them didn't mind. But there were a few others who always squawked. They were too square, but I played the records anyway!

As luck would have it though, when it came time for Chet and his quartet to begin his month at Birdland, I was working the top part of the swing shift, 6 a.m. to 12 p.m. - which meant that by the time it came around for Chet to be playing his two weeks opposite Miles Davis, I'd be working the 6 p.m. to midnight the first week and the midnight to 6 a.m. shift the second week. Unless I could find someone to swap shifts, I'd not only miss the chance to see Chet again, but also miss the chance to sit in and play with him and his group. To say that I was frantic would be an understatement. I called the other two guys who worked the swing shift, and asked each one if they'd be willing to swap their shifts with me for the last two weeks of the month, but unfortunately for me, they could not for each had made plans of their own. So that March night of 1954 in Boston turned out to be the last time I would see Chet for the next fourteen years.

Chapter 2
Reunion at Donte's

After my missed opportunity to see Chet again at Birdland, life pretty much went back to normal. I was still working the swing shift at the paper mill, played drums when I could. One night while making a phone call, a sexy voiced operator asked, 'Number please' and instead of giving her one, I just started talking to her. We became intrigued with each other and spent the next couple hours on the phone. The next Saturday, we met at a local dance hall and wound up dancing the night away. She was tall, blonde and very pretty. We fell in love and were married. A few months into the marriage, I felt the urge to play again, to go on the road, to see if I could make something of myself, something my dear dad never had the chance to do. My wife was strong, grounded and settled and I learned too late that I wasn't ready to settle down, wanting to travel and play drums, whenever and wherever I could. It was over quickly and we divorced. I had no regrets though because from our union God had blessed us with a beautiful daughter, Karen Marie.

And then, sometime later I happened to drop by Birdland. While I was there a young woman was asked to come up on stage. Well, she sang one of the most difficult tunes to sing; a very rangy song called *Midnight Sun*, and she knocked me out! I asked the bartender who she was and found out she was just 'sitting in.' I looked around the club for her later but she'd vanished. I left the club believing I would never see her again. And yet, a couple of years later, my sister Pauline told me she'd seen a pretty blonde girl on local television who was appearing in Portland, Maine with her group and would be there for a week. I was curious, so I went in that night to check her out. To my surprise, it was the same girl, Earla Porch, and she was singing the exact same song. This time, when she came down off the stage, I immediately introduced myself to her, and the rest, as they say, is history. We fell in love and I moved to Cambridge, Massachusetts, where Earla lived. Several months later we were married.

We both loved Chet Baker's music. Although I didn't hear much news about him, I played Chet's music every day. There was something about it that was spiritual. I did know that he was touring in Europe and someone told me Chet was on drugs. That flabbergasted me. Chet had never even smoked when we had met just a few years ago. I said, nah, but this friend said Chet was a drug addict. Hearing that kind of pissed me off. Still, I didn't care what people said about him, his music was like a magnet. I just had to listen to this guy play.

Earla and I didn't stay long in Cambridge, and moved back to Maine. I started my own group, *Art Frank and the Jazz Jets*. The group was all black; I was the only white. We were like brothers, very tight. We played a couple of gigs, and like most struggling jazz musicians, I had a job to make ends meet -- driving a yellow taxicab. However, the band broke up because we couldn't get much work. It was still the '50s, and I suppose civil rights hadn't made it to Portland yet. Our son, Arthur,II, was born in 1958 and by '59 I was fed up driving a cab, so Earla and I moved back to Cambridge. I played in clubs all around Boston, and in Newport. This time, I took a job as a janitor in Boston to feed my family. I still didn't hear much about Chet, unless it was a new record, which I always purchased.

During this time, I also did some acting. I played the lead in a production of the Terence Rattigan play, *Separate Tables*. Earla loved my acting and convinced me to give it shot out in Hollywood. She stayed in Cambridge at her mom's, along with our son. I knew a guy named Ray Sampson, who was from California and asked if I could ride back with him. This was in 1960. Another friend told me when I was out in L.A. to look up his uncle, John Feeney, known professionally as John Ford, the film director. I didn't believe him at first, but he assured me this was his uncle and he'd meet with me. His name was actually John Martin Feeney. I took him up on his suggestion.

Once in Hollywood, I met a number of producers and did read for John Ford. He wanted me to do a picture that starred

Richard Widmark, Ricardo Montalban and James Stewart called *Cheyenne Autumn*. Mr. Ford also sent me over to Batjac Productions founded by John Wayne. He thought I had a good look for movies. He asked if I could ride a horse, and I, of course, said yes! It had only been a few months in L.A. when I received a telegram from home, telling me my father was sick. He suffered from emphysema and it looked pretty bad. I put everything about acting on hold and hurried back to Maine. The good news was that my dad rallied and when he was out of danger, I went down to Cambridge to be with Earla and our son. Soon after, our daughter Rhonda was born in 1961. Then, in early1963, Earla encouraged me to give it another shot in Hollywood, so the four us moved out west.

I picked up where I left off. I called John Ford and he recommended I work in television, but that's not what I wanted. I actually didn't believe television would last!

Of course, I needed work, so I started painting houses and odd jobs like that. I kept playing drums, writing songs, but never published them. I would sit in at most of the well-known jazz clubs in L.A., like The IT club, Mr. Adams, and The Intermission clubs on Washington Blvd.; Redd Fox's place on LaCienega, Shelly's Manne Hole on Yucca in Hollywood, Donte's and Ellis Island in North Hollywood, The Lighthouse in Hermosa Beach, Marty's On The Hill on La Brea, Willie Davis's Center Field in Baldwin Hills, The Playboy Club on Sunset Blvd., and The Flying Fox and Memory Lane, both located on Santa Barbara Ave. (now Martin Luther King, Jr. Blvd.). It was still swingin' in L.A. then, before rock and roll took over the scene.

Then the telegram came again, and this time my Dad couldn't rally. He died on February 28, 1964. I couldn't go back to Maine. Not because everything was great in L.A., in fact we didn't have much money at the time. The reality was, like I told my mother, I couldn't bear to see my father in a coffin.

I continued playing here and there with different groups until the jazz club scene began drying up due to the heavy influx of rock 'n' roll music. A lot of great jazz musicians suddenly found themselves out of work. There were still a few clubs open in

New York City, but only the names were getting any work. It wasn't that much better in Los Angeles, even though I did get to play with a lot of great musicians. In '65 I decided to move back to Westbrook to be with my mother and other family members.

I had very little money left when we arrived in Westbrook. A friend of mine told me about this little cabin on the outskirts of Westbrook and the owner was only asking $150.00 a month. I called the owner, who assured us that it would be as warm as toast in the winter, so without bothering to check it out, we paid the money and rented the place, sight unseen.

The cabin was situated about 300 yards off the main road, and the road leading to it was totally unpaved. When we got to the cabin and opened the door, there was only this one long room about 15 feet long with a full-length drape separating an adjoining room about 7 feet long which had a small bathroom with a tiny bathtub and sink. The place was completely without any type of insulation. There was a kitchen stove, which ran on oil. And man, didn't that ever smell during the long cold winter months.

We fashioned a bedroom for Earla and the two kids and I used the old couch for my bed. The one saving grace we had through those unbelievably long, cold winter months was a small portable record player I had brought with us from L.A. All it played was 45rpm records. And the only 45rpms I happened to have was a Pacific Jazz Chet Baker record, which I still have in my possession to this very day. The tunes on the record were, *The Lamp is Low, Maid in Mexico, Imagination*, and *Russ Job*. I played that record over and over and over, every day and night, and never got sick of it. Listening to those records made me dream. On one of those cold winter days, Earla was sitting by the stove, in her robe.

"I'm so sick of this place," she said.

"Summer's coming, I'll be able to get work," I told her. One of Chet's records was playing, as usual. I wanted to cheer Earla up, comfort her somehow, so I made her a promise.

"One day, I'll have Chet playing for us in our own living room." That promise gave me hope, it made me dream that there was still something else I could accomplish. If you have nothing to hope for you may as well be dead.

After many months at that cabin, I was able to move my family back to Los Angeles. It was 1967, and by the time the summer of '68 rolled around, I'd been playing gigs with a lot of great musicians, such as jazz pianist, Phil Moore III, jazz organist extraordinaire, Richard "Groove" Holmes, vibraphonist great, Roy Ayers, tenor/soprano great, Curtis Amy, bassist giant, Herbie Lewis, guitarist Thornell Schwartz, perhaps the greatest octave jazz guitarist in history, Harry "Sweets" Edison, and King Pleasure at the famed Memory Lane on Santa Barbara Blvd; also, the absolutely fantastic tenor saxophonist, Harold Land, and many others.

It was a strange and sad summer in 1968. I'll never forget that awful June night when Robert Kennedy was shot by Sirhan Sirhan in the kitchen of the Ambassador Hotel on Wilshire Blvd. and the announcement of Kennedy's death the following day. I remember that night with deep sorrow, as I do the horrible assassinations of his brother, John, President of the United States, and Dr. Martin Luther King. The years between 1963 and 1970 were fraught with uncertainty. And, it was in those same years that I would reunite with Chet Baker and become his friend and drummer.

On a night sometime in late June or early July, I was on my way to a jazz club in North Hollywood to sit in with Groove Holmes. While driving along Lankershim Boulevard, I happened to look across the street to check out the marquee at Donte's, a small jazz club near Universal Pictures Studio. I nearly flipped out when I saw Chet Baker's name written across the front. Without thinking or worrying about traffic, I abruptly swung the car into a parking lot across the street from the club, very nearly hitting the fire hydrant in my excitement. I parked and ran across the street to the club. As I neared the entrance, I could hear the unmistakable tone that only Chet Baker could make, with one glaring exception: there wasn't any strength in it.

I walked inside just as he finished playing and lowered the horn to his knee. I walked over to the bar and got myself a beer, then made it over to a table directly in front of the small raised bandstand and sat down. I glanced around the room. Unlike the last time I'd seen Chet in Boston at the jam-packed Storyville, this place was empty except for maybe four couples. I looked up to the stand and saw Chet seated in a chair with his eyes closed tightly and his left leg folded over his right, his head leaning forward, resting on the hand holding the trumpet. Somehow, he looked so small up there.

The rhythm section players were really happening. When the piano player finished his solo, the bassist took a chorus, and then Chet started to play. I couldn't believe my ears. His sound was weak, tentative and unsure, like he had nothing left. On top of that, he looked gaunt, thinner and not quite as agile as I remembered him, and that concerned me. I couldn't quite figure out what was wrong. He wasn't playing well and didn't seem like his old self. It was then I realized that what I'd been hearing about Chet being on drugs was true. Even if he was, I was just so thankful to God that I had run into him again and I knew it was no accident.

I stood up and waved to him but he really couldn't see me because of the lighting overhead on the stand. He ended his solo and brought the tune to an end. Chet came down off the stand and went over to a table a few feet away from me. He was immediately engaged in conversation with one of the couples. I was truly excited to see him again after so many years, and yet, I felt sadness in my heart seeing him the way he was now. He left the couple and made his way in a direct line toward my table, and walked right by me.

I called out his name and he stopped, looked back and came to my table with a curious look on his face. I knew he didn't recognize or remember me, so I decided to see if he'd remember the conversation we'd once had outside Storyville in '54. I asked if he remembered when he'd told me how if he hadn't been a trumpet player, he would have liked to have driven a car at Le Mans and win. He just stood there quietly reflecting, until smile broke out across his face, and said softly that he did recall the night, and asked how I was doing. I told him I was doing okay, but was more interested in knowing if he was going to be playing in the club again the following night.

"No, no. I won't be here tomorrow," he answered. "The owner was nice enough to give me a gig, but..." He stopped, shrugged his shoulders. "Said I wasn't pulling in enough business, so he let me go."

I didn't understand why anyone in their right mind wouldn't want to have the likes of Chet Baker working their club regardless of how he played, or how much business he was doing. "What do you mean? You're Chet Baker! You could play in any club on earth."

"Well, I suppose at one time that was true." He stopped abruptly and with a hint of sadness in his eyes looked beyond me. "No... not anymore, man. Not anymore," he replied, his voice trailing off.

I stood there studying him trying to understand exactly why he was in the shape he was in. "Why? I don't get it?"

"Well, I haven't really been playing all that much for the last couple of years now, man. Just can't do it anymore." The weariness in his voice was heavy. "I sing more than I play."

When he said that, I felt a deep sadness. I truly wanted to reach out to him. This man's music had brought so much beauty into my life. So, I asked him what was going on. He reached up and placed his hand over his mouth, "No chops! Everything's gone! No upper teeth left." He opened his mouth and removed a cheap looking partial plate and held it in the palm of his hand, then brought his other hand up to the side of his upper left cheek and ran it down along side of his jaw.

"Got permanent nerve damage to my mouth and jaw, too," he said. "I'm not the same player I used to be, man. Don't know if I ever will be either." He paused thoughtfully. "If I can't be... I'll probably just..." He let the thought die on his tongue.

I hadn't had any idea as to the seriousness and depth of what he was telling me, but I could certainly see the look of fear and anguish on his face. He was sincerely concerned and also truly scared about the prospects of never being able to play again.

"What? What'd'ya mean, Chet?" I asked.

"It's a long story, man," he replied softly.

I could sense he was tired and probably couldn't wait to get home and into bed, but I didn't want to let him go. "I've got time, Chet," I said with genuine interest.

"Maybe some other time, man," he said solemnly. Before I could ask him another question, the club owner called out and said he was locking up the place. Chet excused himself, walked to the bandstand, got his horn, said goodnight to the owner, and left the club. I was right behind him.

Once outside, I figured he'd give me the proverbial, polite, 'nice to have seen you again bit,' and leave me standing there. But he didn't, so I took the initiative, and asked him another question.

"You married, Chet?"

"Yeah, I sure am," he answered with beaming pride. "And I've got three wonderful kids, two boys and a girl, and my beautiful wife, Carol."

I told him I was married, and also had three kids, two girls and a boy, just the opposite of what he had.

"I was thinking, if you're not doing anything special tomorrow night, I'd love to have you and your wife come over to my little house in Culver City to have dinner with me and my family."

He regarded me with curious suspicion. The look in his eyes told me he was trying to figure out what I was up to. Why was I inviting him and his wife to my house for dinner? I could sense right then and there that he was on his guard and didn't trust anybody.

"Well… I appreciate the offer and all, man. But I really don't know that much about you. And, my wife and I keep pretty much to ourselves. We don't go out very much, you know?"

It didn't take much for me to figure out that this was his way of gently letting me know that his answer was NO.

"So I guess I'm just going to have to pass, man," he said quietly and extended his hand. We shook hands, and he continued. "Maybe we can get together again sometime."

He proceeded to explain to me how he had met hundreds of different people and could hardly remember any one of them. I told him I understood, and reached for my pack of cigarettes and offered him one. He took one and I held my cigarette lighter under his until it was lit. He took a long drag and blew the smoke out slowly. He took another drag and asked how long I'd been in Los Angeles with my family, and what my plans were.

As we stood there talking, I got the feeling that he was beginning to warm up to me and I felt really good about that. Then, out of the blue, he changed his mind and told me that he had decided to take me up on my offer. He would bring Carol to my house for dinner the next night. Delighted, I told him I'd set up everything with my wife and give him a call to let him know the time. I asked for his telephone number.

"I don't have a phone, man. The phone company shut off my service two weeks ago."

I couldn't believe it. I was shocked that a man of such worldwide fame and musical acclaim didn't even have a working telephone. I felt bad for him but tried hard not to show it. I wrote 'Drummer, Art Frank' and my phone number down on the back of one of my painting business cards and asked him to call me the next day. He smiled and promised he would. We stood there for another few minutes talking, then went our separate ways.

Chapter 3
Promise Fulfilled

On the drive home, my mind was deluged with thoughts about Chet. I didn't know why at the time, but I decided to start taking mental notes and writing things down about Chet. It was weird because I'd met and played with just about every bop/jazz luminary by the time I was twenty, and not once did I ever feel compelled to write down things about them. Hell, I never so much as asked for an autograph, or to have my picture taken with any of them, not even the great Charlie Parker. But I really felt led to begin writing, taping and memorizing everything I could about Chet, including my first and second meeting with him.

By the time I got home, it was nearly 2 o'clock in the a.m. and Earla was sound asleep. I was much too excited about having run into Chet, so I woke her up and told her all about everything that happened and how I had invited him and his wife over for dinner. She was ecstatic, jumped up out of bed, started trying to figure just what we could get for dinner on the amount of money we had left, which was not a hell of a lot.

All during the next day, Earla wouldn't allow anyone to use the phone. And when any calls came in, she made sure the caller was off within seconds. That's how thrilled and excited she was. She kept that line open all day long until finally Chet called in the middle of the afternoon and confirmed they'd be coming over for dinner. Man, we were both thrilled and excited beyond our wildest dreams.

I really didn't have any money to speak of at the time. I had been doing a lot of house painting in between gigs because that gave me the chance to earn more bread than I could playing drums. However, on that particular week I wasn't getting paid until the middle of the following week. So we sat down and counted the money we did have. It amounted to exactly 14 dollars and 71 cents. We didn't know what the hell we were going to do, or exactly how the hell we were going to do it. And then I was struck with an idea. We could leave the kids with my cousin, Bunky and his wife Lorraine for the night. I ran it by Earla -- she was all for it.

I went to the local variety store on West Washington Blvd., just around the corner from where we lived on Caroline Ave. The owner of the market knew me well because his was the only store in the neighborhood where we bought our food, and yet, the cheap bastard wouldn't allow me to get anything on credit. So I bought what I could with the 14 bucks I had: four pounds of sirloin steak, it was pretty cheap then, a five pound bag of Maine potatoes, a couple of cans of string beans, a big Dutch apple pie, a quart of vanilla ice cream and four slices of cheese in the event Chet and Carol might like it on their pie instead of ice cream. I tried to think of everything I could get that would please Chet. I wanted him to have a good meal and then feel comfortable enough around me that he'd want to sit around for a while afterwards so that we could get to know each other better.

Five o'clock came and went. Chet hadn't shown up. This made Earla very nervous. "Do you really think he's going to come, Art?" she asked anxiously. "He'll come, I'm sure of it. He said he'd come and I believe he will." Assured by what I'd said, Earla started setting the table, which in this instance, wasn't actually a table, but a long counter measuring approximately seven feet long by four feet wide - perfect for four.

Six o'clock came and went. Still, no Chet. Earla was dubious that they'd ever show up, but I never doubted for a moment. I went over to the window next to the front door and peered outside at every car that drove by the house. Finally, after another ten minutes or so, a car pulled up in front and parked. Two people got out. "It's Chet! He's here, Earla!" I shouted happily, and ran to open the door.

There stood Chet Baker and this beautiful, raven-haired woman. "This is my wife, Carol," he said softly. I took her hand warmly and invited them inside. At first I thought she was quite a bit like Chet because she seemed to be so quiet and reserved, but soon found out that once she felt comfortable she opened up, speaking with a buoyant English accent.

After dinner, the four of us opened a bottle of wine and listened to some of Chet's records on the record player. I settled back and set out to discover who each one of us were. I had asked Chet to bring along his horn; thankfully he had, and offered to try and play something for us.

He excused himself and went out to the car and came back carrying a light blue chenille bath towel and set it on the counter, then slowly began to unwrap it, revealing a Bach flugelhorn. He reached into his pocket, took out a mouthpiece and placed it onto the barrel of the horn and then seated himself on the edge of the couch. He leaned forward a bit, placed his left leg over his right knee, lifted the horn to his lips, and played a few notes.

I looked across the room to Earla, who was in conversation with Carol, and caught her attention. I gestured to her indicating my great excitement. Through God's grace, the promise I'd made to Earla on that cold winter day back in Maine was being fulfilled. Chet Baker was in our home about to play.

Chet raised the horn back up to his lips and fingered the three valves in rapid sequence, blew into the mouthpiece, stopped to adjust the partial plate, then started rubbing his mouth and side of his face. Concerned, I asked him what was wrong, but he didn't answer. Instead, he rubbed his cheek and jaw again, grimaced slightly, and then told us that whenever he tried to play he felt pain. At times his mouth and the whole side of his face would go numb.

There is one important thing I came to understand about the embouchure, the particular way a musician applies the facial muscles of the mouth and tongue around the mouthpiece. If your chops are down, you can sound great for about five minutes and then your tone sounds terrible. This is because the muscles fatigue and you can't hold that certain set of muscles tight without wavering or dropping off a note.

Chet rubbed the side of his cheek for a minute or so, then lifted the horn to his lips and tried again. I ran to the closet to dig out my old reel-to-reel tape recorder and came right back and set it up on the counter, and said another prayer that it would run. I plugged the cord in, flicked the switch and both reels began to spin. It worked! My prayers had again been answered and another dream was about to come true.

Chet brought the horn up to his mouth, and I quickly hit record to tape this momentous moment. He played the tune *I Love You* from his *Chet Baker & Strings* album. At first he sounded pretty good. But about half way through the tune his embouchure gave out. He winced in pain and rubbed the side of his mouth with the palm of his hand. He looked weary, lowered the horn onto his lap, and with a long sigh, looked over to Carol, discouraged.

Not wanting to push him any further I turned off the tape recorder.

We had another cup of coffee after which he said he wanted to try to play again. He got the flugelhorn and I turned my tape recorder on. He made another attempt and managed to play some of the melody before having to stop and rest. "No chops!" he said frustrated and tried again. This time he was able to play a melodic scale of 8th notes (a scale of thirds), but soon ran out of steam and pulled the horn away from his mouth and rested it on his knee, and sighed, "Oh… that's the most I've played... That's the most I've played in weeks."

We all laughed appreciatively, so happy for him that he'd found the strength to play as much as he could for us. I'll never forget that moment. I watched him with quiet awe and some sadness while he put the horn back into the towel, rolled it tightly and placed it under his chair.

Life is so strange, I thought then. Here was Chet Baker, one the greatest trumpet players that ever lived and he's unable to play with the same grace, dexterity and fluidity that had made him famous. Sitting at my kitchen table, he seemed so vulnerable. I couldn't help but be reminded of my dad. I remembered him sitting at the kitchen table in front of the wood stove, dressed at dawn to go to work. My dad loved jazz and wanted to make a career of it, but every day he worked at the mill to pay the rent, buy wood for the stove, pay the electricity bill and buy food to feed nine mouths.

And still, at our house, even through the years of the Depression, there was always laughter, a few tears, and a whole lot of music, especially jazz. No matter how rough things got, even when we only had baked Spam and a slice of pineapple for Thanksgiving dinner, there was my father, playing his C melody sax. Yeah, my dad wanted to be in it, but he died and never got the chance to see if he could have made it.

Now, sitting here with Chet, I made up my mind to center my attention on getting him back into playing music again full time. I needed to find out how and what I could do to help this God-gifted jazz musician keep playing the music he and I loved.

Chapter 4
Getting to Know Chet

I poured more coffee and asked Chet if he would mind if I did a taped interview with him, like a kind of a spoof live radio bit. He smiled and said he wouldn't mind, so I again set the tape recorder up on the kitchen counter and began the interview:

> "We have the distinct pleasure of having Chet Baker in our house this evening. Let's see if I can get Chet Baker to say a few words into the microphone? Chet!"

Chet leaned forward, put his mouth close to the microphone and spoke in a playful mock growl:

> *"Hey, yeah, Baby... I'm real happy to be here tonight. I dig your show... real hip show."*
>
> "How long have you been digging the show, Chet?"
>
> *"Well... I hardly ever listen to my radio at home, you know? I haven't really heard the show."*
>
> "I've been told by thousands of fans of yours that you're one of our most ardent listeners. This comes as quite a shock to hear that you don't listen to your radio, Chet!"
>
> *"Well... you know how people like to bullshit all of the time,"*
>
> "YES, but we spin one of your records at least once a year!"
>
> *"Well... I thank you for that. Wish it could be*

more."

"Well, no one from payola has come around in the last six months."

"Well, times are bad baby! Reeeeaaalll bad!"

Chet's tone had become a bit more serious. He was acutely aware of his own condition, and of his not being able to play good enough to make a living to support his wife and family. I could see the inner hurt and wanted to keep things light.

"I'm hip. But have you ever thought of any other means, Chet, of having an outlet for your creative abilities, as it were, besides playing the flugelhorn and the trumpet?"

"Well, I've thought of armed robbery...."

We all laughed at that, breaking the tension. Earla asked about his children, which helped to keep things going. I picked up from there.

"I understand that you're married?"

"Yes, that's right! I am married, and I've got three....monsters."

We laughed again. Chet had a unique way of laughing. He would inhale his breath, staccato like, as though gasping for air, and the sound would come from the back of his throat. Other times, he'd do it in reverse.

"Well, the little girl is not really a monster. She's...

"Melissa isn't it?"

"Yeah. We call her Missy, Sissy, Sassy..."

"And, what are you doing right now, Chet? Besides sitting at our table, drinking coffee?"

"Not too much, man! [sighs] Not too much goin' on."

"I understand that you just recently bought yourself a Cadillac, Chet?"

"Nooo, nooo, my mother bought that for me."

He said this with such childlike innocence that Earla commented to Carol on how honest Chet was to admit that.

"Tell me Chet, do you think all this honesty pays off?"

"Nooo, I'm sure it doesn't!"

"Well, have you ever thought of perpetrating any other ideas?"

"In regard to honesty?"

"Yeah…"

"Well, I've thought about it, but ah… I just don't seem to be able to… to pull it off, you know?"

"Now, I understand you're somewhat of an artist? That you've painted several pictures in your lifetime?"

"Ummm, well, when I was in the neuro-psychiatric ward in the Army Hospital, up in Letterman, I used to draw. Weird… weird pictures, man."

"I understand that while you were in Paris, you had two, not one, but both of your trumpets stolen from you, is that right?"

"That is correct. One was taken out of the kitchen at the 'Chat Qui Peche' in Paris, and one was taken right off the piano… I don't remember the name of the club, in Naples."

He went on to tell me how terribly much he liked Italy. If he had the chance to go back, he said he'd go just as fast as he could and had his attorney working on it.

"Why do you find it so much more interesting in Italy, than here in America?"

> *"Ooooh, it... the living over there gives you such a feeling of being FREEEE! Reeeally freeee! I don't know what it is. I really can't explain it."*
>
> "Just a sense of freedom, as it were, right Chet?"
>
> *"That's it. You know, the people over there are so warm. Such great people."*

I then shifted the interview to Carol. "Mrs. Baker, would you like to ask your husband a question?" She, being quite shy, shook her head in the negative.

"Into the microphone, love," Chet coaxed. She said no, and he began to chuckle, "Why don't you say a few words?" And again, she shied away. So, I added to the coaxing, hoping to get a reaction from her.

> "C'mon, Carol. We want to get some of your English brogue on here."
>
> *"The English don't have brogues!"*

Earla then suggested that she say something about their children. And that turned out to be the springboard needed to get her to loosen up and talk. And then Chet began talking about his youngest son, Paul.

> *"Paul got lost today."*
>
> "Who found him?"
>
> *"The police found him!"*
>
> *"Yes, Dean lost him! Paul tagged along behind Dean, and somehow got lost." (Carol)*
>
> *"We were so scared, we had to call the police, and thankfully, they found him in a park about a mile from our house." (Chet)*

Chet let out a long sigh of relief. Carol smiled and echoed his sentiments. It was easy to see they both loved their kids.

Earla asked Carol if she wanted another cup of tea, and before she could answer, an uncontrollable yawn escaped her mouth. She hurriedly covered her mouth with her hand and apologized, then asked what time it was getting to be. It was only 9:45 so I asked if they could stay a while longer. I reminded Chet that he hadn't yet had a piece of the Dutch apple pie I had bought, hoping that would entice them to stay.

"You can have a slice of cheddar cheese or vanilla ice cream...."

Chet looked at Carol and smiled.

"You know how much I like apple pie and ice cream, Carol."

She looked at him stone-faced for a few seconds then smiled. I got up and quickly went to the refrigerator and grabbed the big pie, the box of ice cream and served out some for each of us. We spent the next few minutes in sheer delight eating our pie and ice cream. Chet looked so happy and contented, like a little boy who had done a good deed and was now happily eating his reward. As soon as we finished our desert I got up and made another cup of coffee for Chet, and me and a cup of tea for Carol.

Chapter 5
The Brutal Beating

Earla was a dress designer as well as a jazz vocalist, visual artist and sculptor. She wanted to show Carol some of her works so the two of them went into the den, which also served as our master bedroom. Chet sat at the table finishing his coffee. He had a distant look on his face. It seemed as if he was feeling some kind of an aching pain, not just in his jaw, but also in his heart. I wanted to know what was causing it, and if I could help in any way. I also really wanted to know what had happened to cause him to play so terribly weak.

"You said that you had lost all of your chops, Chet. Is that really true?"

"Well, yeah, I pretty much have," he answered softly.

"Were you in an accident or something?"

"More like a fuckin' earthquake, man," he said, and opened his mouth and moved the loose fitting partial plate from side-to-side with ease.

"It's a partial," he said and moved it back and forth again. "Too damn loose, keeps falling out whenever I try to play." He lit a cigarette and inhaled deeply. "I lost these four upper front teeth about a year and a half ago when I was attacked and beaten up by five black hoodlums."

"You gotta be shitting me? Where, man?" I asked, shocked and surprised.

I remembered when I'd first seen him in Boston back in 1954 he already had a missing upper front tooth. Vera, Chet's mother, would later relate to me how Chet had accidentally lost that tooth in his early teens. She talked about how one afternoon after school, while living in Glendale, California, Chet and a couple of his classmates had been throwing rocks up at the overhead street light, when one of the rocks happened to ricochet off the metal reflector surrounding the bulb, hitting Chet directly on the upper left front tooth, dislodging it immediately. That was how he had lost the tooth.

"No... no," Chet answered. "I'm not kidding. They did a hell of a job on me, man."

I was about to ask him another question about it when Carol, who had apparently heard our conversation, came rushing back into the room seething. She really couldn't contain her anger and started to tell Earla and me all about what had happened to Chet. She told us the five young hoodlums had done a hell of a lot more than just beat Chet up.

Chet had been mauled by the five of them, and the thought of it seemed to build her anger. They had beaten him up so severely and brutally, that if it hadn't of been for the two nice black men who had come to Chet's aid, Chet probably would have been beaten to death, right then and there.

Carol lit up a cigarette, her face still taut over the thought of what had happened to Chet.

"Did you know who the pricks were?" I asked.

"Not personally. I'd seen them hanging around the club from time to time."

"What club was that?"

"The Trident, a jazz club in Sausalito." He stopped, cleared his throat. "Anyway, they knew I was an addict... and somehow they had found out I was getting paid that night... So, they waited in the alley beside the club until I came out, and then came at me like gangbusters. They made a circle around me and demanded I give them my bread." He stopped, took a long drag off his cigarette and exhaled. "I told them to go fuck themselves and get a job and earn their own fuckin' bread. And, WHAM, WHAM, BOOM those five mother-fuckers were all over me at once." With that he unconsciously started rubbing his cheek and jaw again.

"Sons-a-bitches!! Wish I'd have been there."

"I wish you had of been, too," he said. "They knocked me to the ground and started punching and kicking me in the head, the face, my stomach, my balls and all over my legs. I covered my face as best I could but it didn't do much good."

"Where the hell were all the cops, man?" I asked.

Carol, still a little upset over the whole episode, indicated that there were no policemen anywhere.

"They would have killed me if--"

Carol asked Chet to tell us about how a white couple had witnessed his being kicked and punched continually while he was on the ground and then drove away. Her face clearly showed her disgust.

"When I saw a car coming toward me and stopping, I managed to stand up somehow and break away to run over to the car. There was a middle age white couple and they had their two teenage kids with them sitting in the back seat. I tried to open the rear door to get in but those two kids, both boys, wouldn't let me in. They pushed me away from the car with their feet and shut the door and yelled for their father to take off, which he did, leaving me there to die."

"Yellow bastards!" I said. "How could anyone turn their backs on a fellow man like that?" It was very troubling to me, but I had to know more. "Did those guys come after you again?"

"Yeah, and just as they started to beat me again, a big black Ford sedan pulled up a few feet away and parked and we all thought they were cops. These two big black men get out dressed in business suits and started walking over toward us. Well, those five bastards tore off out of that alley like they'd been shot out of a shotgun, each going his own way into the night."

"Were they cops?"

"No," Chet laughed. "Just two guys on their way home from work. They thought I was going to die right then and there so they helped me to their car and drove me to the nearest hospital. I guess they didn't want any attention drawn to them so they pulled up to the front of the Emergency ward door and waited until they caught the attention of some nurse and then drove away."

"God bless them, man. They were probably angels sent by God."

"Yeah, I probably wouldn't be here today if those two cats hadn't have come along when they did."

"Ever find out who they were Chet?"

"No… No, I never saw them again. I think about them every

now and then though, you know?" He rubbed his cheek again and looked past me reflectively. "The doctors told me that in their opinion I'd never play trumpet again, and that I should look for some other way to make a living. Well… I couldn't just sit around so I got a job in a gas station pumping gas and washing windshields for a while, you know?"

They explained how the doctors told Chet he'd suffered permanent trigeminal nerve damage to both sides of his face and jawbone and that in their professional opinion, he would have it for the rest of his life.

"What does that mean?"

"Well… when I play on a steady basis, IF and when I ever do, then it's going to cause pain and numbness around my cheeks and mouth. When the doctors said that, it really scared the hell out of me," he said quietly. He exhaled a long painful sigh. "Playing is all I really know how to do, and not being able to play trumpet again… Well…" He left the thought unfinished.

"Man, what'd you do when the doctors told you?"

"Well, I wasn't about to give up, so I took odd jobs here and there to pay bills and put food on our table. The kids had to have a place to live, and Carol wouldn't let me give up either. She encouraged me to pick up the horn and keep on trying...."

Carol's feelings about the odd jobs Chet took on were clear. She couldn't stand watching him pumping gas and washing windshields and having people drive up and asking him to check their tires for air, and things like that. It wasn't because she thought Chet was above doing that sort of work… she insisted that she just didn't want him to give up his desire to want to play trumpet again.

"I'm not going to, love."

"How long ago did it happen?" I asked.

"Well, let's see…" He looked to Carol. "You had just given birth to Missy, what, the night before, right?"

As it was, their daughter was born on the 22nd of July, 1966 and Chet's beating took place the following night. Still feeling drained from giving birth, Carol had received a call from a nurse in a different hospital informing her that Chet had been attacked and was being cared for by a doctor in their emergency ward. He would be released as soon as he was fit to leave. I could sense

Carol's anger building again as she relived the memory of the ordeal. She hadn't been given a report on the severity of Chet's injuries and was shocked after she saw him. There was no doubt this trauma would affect the lives of Chet and his family from then on.

Listening to her impassioned description of what she had seen, clearly and unmistakably indicated to me that there was still a lot fire burning deep inside her gut. He and Carol exchanged looks as she related the story. It was evident that he had gone through a great deal of pain and suffering, and it was equally evident that she was right there beside him. I'll never forget the unmistakable look of love the two of them exchanged that night. It was really a wonderful thing to witness.

I remember reading in some magazine or newspaper somewhere, that there were a few people who have said the severe beating of Chet Baker had never actually taken place, that he had invented the whole thing in order get sympathy from people, to get money so that he could buy dope. Well, I saw him not that long after that terrible beating, and the results of it were still evident, especially around the mouth area; along with the absence of four upper front teeth, one lost previously as a teenager, the other three as a result of the beating. I also know for a fact that he had suffered permanent trigeminal nerve damage to both cheeks and jaw, because I personally witnessed the pain and numbness it caused him whenever he made the attempt to play.

Carol and Earla moved back into the den while Chet and I remained in the kitchen. I fixed us another cup of coffee and we both lit up a cigarette.

"Man, the thought of never playing again scares the hell out of me. And I know that Carol's really worried, even though she tries not to show it, you know?"

I remember vividly the look on his face when he confided this fear to me. Here was a man who was one of the two greatest lyrical and melodic players of all-time in my opinion, Charlie Parker being the other. Chet's gift and ability to play had been brutally taken away by five non-descript punks for no reason other than to steal his money. This great trumpet genius had absolutely no idea of what he might do if it came to pass that he could never play again. He was seriously concerned.

Chapter 6
Herb Alpert's Thoughtfulness

Over the course of that first evening at my home, I learned from Chet how tough the sixties had been for him to get decent paying gigs. By then, most of the clubs and record companies only wanted to use rock 'n' roll musicians. That made it rough on all the great jazz players to support themselves. 1966 had been an especially lean year for Chet. A few months before he'd suffered the brutal beating, he told me the only person who had really cared enough about him and his family, cared enough to help him earn decent bread, was trumpeter Herb Alpert. When nobody else did, Herb stepped up and signed him to record two Mariachi albums for his company, A&M Records. Chet talked about how much he had sincerely appreciated his help.

"I didn't really care for that type of music," he said softly. "But man… things were rough and the gigs weren't happening… and I really needed the bread to pay the rent and put food on the table for Carol and the kids." He stopped talking and lowered his head for a few seconds. "Herb understood my need and was there for me. That's something I'm never going to forget, you know?"

I was moved by Herb's genuine kindness of heart. As far as I was concerned, what he had done for Chet spoke volumes about the compassion of the man, Herb Alpert!

Listening to Chet tell me about Herb and other things, made me feel damn special. Here he was, sitting in my little home, stripped of his ability to earn a living doing the only thing he loved to do, play jazz. As I sat there trying to absorb everything he was saying, I felt that somehow, some way, through much prayer and encouragement, he was going to play again, and even better than he had before.

"You're not just going to take the doctor's word are you,

Chet?"

"Well... the way I feel when I try to play... kind of makes me believe the doctors know what they're talking about." He paused and then continued. "But no, I really can't... Carol wouldn't dream of letting me give up trying. She encourages me to pick up my horn every day and try to play more and more... to help build up my embouchure, you know?"

Almost as soon as Chet had finished talking about Carol, she walked into the kitchen and stood next to him, a proud smile playing over her face.

She quickly let us know how proud she was of Chet and how much he was going through to rebuild the muscles it would take for him to play trumpet again. She was also very honest about not knowing much about playing a horn or how long it would take. Listening to her talk, I don't think Carol would have been able to live with herself if she didn't do everything she could to help Chet in every way.

I could see tears glistening in her eyes, the unmistakable evidence of her love. Chet put his arm around her and drew her closer.

"Well, it's not going to happen overnight, love. It may take a couple years... and, well... there's no guarantee," he said wearily and shrugged.

I could see that Chet was getting tired and Carol was probably concerned about getting home and didn't want to appear rude, so I suggested it by looking up to the wall clock and affecting a yawn. It worked because all four of us started yawning simultaneously.

"Well, we'd better get going, Carol. My mother's probably wondering where we are. By the way, Art," Chet said, "Here's our home address in case you and Earla want to come down some afternoon to meet our kids." He handed me a piece of paper, and I put it on the front of the refrigerator so I wouldn't lose it. I walked them to the door and we exchanged good nights.

Chapter 7
An Errand in Watts

Four or five days later, I was in my car headed for Chet's house in Redondo Beach. He had called from a neighbor's phone that morning to ask if I could come down and pick him up. He didn't have his Mom's Mustang, and needed to go on some kind of errand. I told him I'd be there around ten o'clock. So there I was, on my way to Chet's house. It was one of those beautiful, warm Southern California mornings where you could see the surrounding mountains off in the distance and smell the scent of cedar trees and chlorine pools. I was especially happy and carefree on this morning because the musician who had inspired me so much over the years and influenced my love of jazz had brought his wife over to my house for dinner, and now, here I was on my way to his house.

I followed his directions carefully and found myself on Spreckles Lane. I continued down the street until I came to the address number he'd given me, 1610, and pulled over and parked the car. The houses were pretty much identical to all the other houses in the area, with the exception of the colors. I parked and walked to the door and noticed a small nameplate, which read CHESNEY H. BAKER. What a strange name that was I thought to myself. I knocked on the door and within seconds, Carol was there with a big smile on her face.

She invited me in and the first thing I noticed was the living room, which must have been at least 35 or 40 feet long with a fireplace and mantle along the far end of the wall where Chet was seated at a small kitchen table. He looked up and seemed genuinely happy to see me, asking if I'd had any trouble finding his house. I told him his directions had been solid. I walked over to the table and was about to sit down when something on the mantle grabbed my attention.

I moved closer and saw two plaque trophies. I picked them up and read the inscriptions on each. They were First Place Downbeat and Metronome poll plaques, which had been given to jazz musicians who placed first in specific categories for the preceding year. Chet had received two.

I was really impressed and told him how great I thought it was to have received something like that. He merely fluffed the whole thing off with nonchalance.

"They don't mean anything, Art. That whole poll thing is pretty much based on popularity rather than on a musician's ability to improvise, you know?" he said in a matter-of-fact tone.

"Maybe," I shot back, "but to me, any musician who could win two national first polls in jazz has to be a hell-of-a-lot-more than just popular! He'd have to really be somethin' else."

"Well, I don't think I really should have won those polls because there are a few players out there who were much more deserving than I was then. Cats like Dizzy and Miles. I mean, I think they were better players than I was at that time," he said softly.

He bowled me over with his simple honesty and lack of ego. I know that if I had won back-to-back first place polls, I would have been bragging about it, that's for sure. But Chet underplayed everything. He walked over to Carol and kissed her.

"Art's taking me to L.A. to see a friend. We should be back in a few hours."

She told Chet to take care, and looked over at me. I got the feeling she wanted me to watch out for him.

I told her I would, then Chet and I left the house, got into my car and headed for the freeway, eventually winding up somewhere in the south central section of Los Angeles.

Chet was very quiet so I just continued driving along the boulevard thinking to myself that he'd tell me where he wanted to go sooner or later. When I came to this one intersection, he suddenly sprang to life.

"Hang a left here and keep driving until you see a small barbershop on the left side of the street, then look for a place to pull over and park."

"OK," I said and continued to drive until I spotted the barbershop. I pulled over, parked and looked around the area, wondering why Chet wanted to stop here. I looked at his head and he didn't look like he was in need of a haircut. Then I recognized the Watts Towers and became pretty damn nervous.

"What are we doing here? We're in Watts, man!" I said, voicing a sincere concern for being in unfamiliar territory where most whites were not welcome. Watts is a residential area located in the south central section of Los Angeles, and is predominantly black. And most of the black people were not very friendly toward the majority of whites.

Just a few months earlier in April 1968, the area was awash in fury and grief after the horrific assassination of Rev. Dr. Martin Luther King, Jr. Also, just three years prior, the area had erupted against growing police intimidation and episodes of brutality that resulted in what came to be known as The Watts Riots. I looked at Chet apprehensively.

"What the hell we doing here, Chet? We could get our asses kicked or a lot worse."

"I know," he said casually. He reached across the seat and tapped my shoulder. "We'll be alright man, don't worry," he calmly assured me. "Nobody's going to fuck with us because most of the people know who I am."

"What does that mean? You want me to go with you?" I asked with concern.

"Yeah, c'mon man, it'll be cool."

I really didn't feel comfortable about going, but because it was Chet, I decided to tag along in case any shit went down and somebody tried to hurt him. I had experience with street fighting and had also done some professional boxing and could handle myself extremely well. We walked across the street and went into the place.

The interior of the barbershop was a dark rose color and the walls were in need of repair and paint. Several posters of jazz musicians lined the walls – Charlie Parker, Dexter Gordon, Billie Holiday, Dizzy Gillespie, Miles Davis and one of Chet. There were three black men inside. The barber was obviously happy to see Chet and asked him what was happening.

"Not too much, Leroy. Not too much, man," he answered softly.

I couldn't help notice Leroy and the other man seated by the window exchanging quick nervous glances, no doubt a little apprehensive by my presence. Chet had also observed their uneasiness and knew just what to do to settle their minds.

"This is my friend Art, Leroy. And he's cool, man, you dig?" Satisfied, Leroy nodded to Chet, then to the man by the window, and went back to cutting the other man's hair, or so it appeared. The more I watched, the more I realized that he wasn't really cutting the man's hair at all, just merely going through the motions because no hair could be seen falling to the floor.

The other black man seated by the window was looking out to the street nervously watching cars drive past. I watched him, trying to figure out what the hell he was up to. He'd watch every car that pulled up and parked, whether it was across the street or next to the barbershop, and check every person, man or woman, who got out. Then it hit me. He was a lookout, and he was looking out for unmarked police cars. What kind of a weird barbershop was this anyway? A fear of the unknown was going round in my brain. Chet immediately picked up on my anxiety and leaned close to my ear and assured me that I had nothing to worry about as far as these three men were concerned.

Leroy either had ESP or had overheard what Chet said to me, and told the other two men that I was also cool. He told me the names of the two men. Nate was the one seated by the window, and Lester was the man seated in the barber's chair getting the fake haircut.

Leroy looked at me, then over to the window, laughed, and told me that Nate was looking out for pig wagons because they didn't want any pig's feet in the place, confirming for me that Nate was indeed on the lookout for police cruisers. He had no more than mentioned that when Nate excitedly yelled out that there were 'pigs on wheels' going slowly by the shop. Leroy reacted and told us to sit down and be cool to make it appear like we were waiting our turn to have our hair cut. He wanted to make sure everything looked on the up-and-up so the police wouldn't see anything suspicious and want to come inside to check him out.

I looked over at Chet and noticed that he was sniffling and rubbing his nose frequently. I'd been told by some of the famous addicts I'd sat in with, this behavior was a sure sign that, unless the person had a cold, it meant they were in need of a fix. That's when I understood that the barbershop was not only a place to get a haircut, but also a front for drug dealers, pushers and users, and that was why Chet was there, to get a fix. And now, I was really concerned and just wanted to get Chet and myself out of there fast.

Leroy told Lester to take over for him while he took Chet with him to show him the new albums he had bought the day before. Lester removed the barber's apron, got out of the chair and took the scissors Leroy handed to him. Lester then told Nate to come over and take his place in the chair, and as soon as he did, Lester covered him with the apron and pretended to cut his hair while Leroy gestured for Chet to follow him.

Chet got up and followed Leroy to the far end of the shop where a long dark green drape hung from the ceiling down to the floor, separating the barber shop from an adjoining back room. Leroy and Chet disappeared behind the drape while I sat there in the chair nervously looking out the window. I turned and looked back toward the curtain, then back at Lester and Nate, who were nervously looking out toward the window to the street. Just then a police cruiser pulled a car over to the curb directly in front of the shop. Lester whipped his head over his shoulder toward the back of the room to inform Leroy that a black 'n' white had stopped out front of the shop and the cop was giving some guy a ticket. Leroy yelled out that he'd be there in a couple minutes.

I was really nervous now. My eyes darted back and forth between the cop and the green drape where Chet was. Finally, after what seemed like an eternity, the cop got back into his cruiser and drove away. Seconds later Chet and Leroy came back out. I immediately noticed that Chet was not in the same physical shape he had been before. He looked weak, and could barely walk. I jumped up and went over and stood between Chet and Leroy.

"Look at him, man, he looks like he just ran a thousand miles. Is he going to be alright?" I asked sharply.

Leroy looked at me with a shit-eating kind of grin and told me not to worry about it, that Chet would be cool in a little while and that I should just drive him home. He said Chet had been hurting real bad and needed some of his special blend, and reiterated that Chet would be cool and back to normal within the hour.

I was pissed. I was also very concerned and wanted to know exactly what, and how much of whatever it was he had given to him. At that time, I didn't really know a hell of lot about drugs and their effect on people so I didn't know if he had given Chet heroin or something else. But I really had no choice but to take his word that Chet would be all right in an hour or so.

I helped Chet to one of the chairs along the wall and sat him down. Then I left the shop and ran across the street to get my car, made a U-turn and parked right in front of the barbershop. I rushed back inside to get Chet. He was now half asleep on the chair. I sat down beside him and asked if he was ready to go. He opened his eyes for a second, closed them again and said he was. I reached under his arm to help him get up but before I could, he stood up suddenly and walked to the door by himself, albeit a bit unsteady. He stopped by the open door, looked back and thanked Leroy, who told Chet that his shop was open to him six days of every week.

"Soup's always on, man," Leroy promised.

"Well… I might be seeing you again in a couple days, man," Chet told him lazily.

Leroy flashed a big smile and answered with the cocksure knowledge that Chet would more than likely have to come back to see him whenever that burning need ripped at his insides. I saw the devious look on Leroy's face and knew that he really didn't give a shit about Chet or for any other poor drug addict.

"No, you're wrong, man! You're never goin' to see Chet here again. Not as long as I'm with him!" I said. "C'mon Chet, let's get the hell out of here before the cops come by and see you looking like this."

I walked him out to the car, got him inside and drove off. I knew about other musicians copping but I'd never seen any of them looking as tired and weak as Chet. Leroy must have given him something pretty damned potent because before long Chet had stretched his weary body out across half the front seat and was sound asleep.

As I drove along all I could do was look at him resting so peacefully and wonder why in God's name he needed to take drugs? Whatever made him start in the first place, I kept asking myself? It really bothered me terribly. Here he was, Chet Baker, my all-time favorite jazz musician and personal inspiration, sitting in the front seat of my car totally unconscious because of some kind of drug. I just couldn't fathom the reason. After several minutes I tried to wake him up but he wouldn't respond, which gave me great cause for concern.

"Chet? Are you alright, man?"

He didn't respond, and I didn't know what the hell to do. A thought hit me that maybe I could scare him awake and see if I would get any kind of reaction.

"CHET, CHET, wake up man! There's a cop tailing us, and he's right on my ass!" It worked. He opened his eyes and started to sit up.

"NO!" I shouted. "Stay low so he won't see you," I said emphatically, and looked into my rear view mirror cautiously, carrying on as though there really was a police car tailing me.

"He's still behind us... so stay where you are," I said nervously, and looked into the rear view mirror again, and let out a long, feigned sigh of relief.

"It's cool now, Chet. Cop's no longer behind us... he just hung a right."

Chet sat up and looked over his shoulder, and then looked at me with a boyish smile full of innocence. I felt it wasn't the right time or circumstance to ask him but I was concerned and needed to know what would have happened if the cops had actually pulled me over.

"I gotta ask you something, Chet. If, for some reason, when we're together, a cop pulls me over after you've had a fix, and sees you stretched out half conscious... there's nothing they could do to me, is there? I mean, they couldn't arrest me or anything, could they?"

"No, they couldn't do a damn thing to you, man! All you're doing is driving. Don't worry about the cops, man," he said and lit up a cigarette. "There's no way I'd ever let anything happen to you, Art."

There was something in his tone that put my mind completely at ease. I absolutely believed that he would never let anything happen to me. Then he became silent and stared blankly at the road up ahead like he was in a trance. After what seemed like an eternity, he broke out of it and wanted me to take him to the beach. I looked at him curiously, and wondered where that idea had come from.

"Which beach, Chet?" I asked. He said it didn't matter, and started to tell me all about how much Charlie Parker loved the beach, and how he always wanted Chet to drive him there. He said how he would sometimes take Bird to Santa Monica Beach, but more often times than not, Bird preferred for long drives around the coastline near Palos Verdes. He loved to get out of the car and walk along the cliffs. Chet told me that Bird would just stand there sometimes for hours looking out over the ocean. Bird liked being around the ocean better than any other spot in the world because it was the only place that he could find peace of mind and feel close to God. He told Chet that if he listened long enough, he'd be able to hear God whisper.

I thought that was pretty amazing. That's exactly how my father felt about being at the ocean. He always used to tell me and my brothers and sisters that no matter how many violent storms take place, or how many different waves crash along the shore, when the storms ended, the oceans, like almighty God, is still there.

"That's probably what Bird saw every time you took him to the beach," I said. Chet didn't say anything, but slowly nodded his head in silent agreement. I asked him again which beach he wanted me to take him to and he said, Santa Monica, because it was the closest to where we were at the time. So we took off and made our way to the beach.

Chapter 8
Santa Monica Confessions

When we arrived at the spot I had in mind, which was just off the main boulevard in the downtown section of Santa Monica, there wasn't a single place to park. I was about to make a U-turn and go all the way back when Chet suddenly spotted a woman getting into her car. I shifted into low gear and pulled up right behind her, sliding smoothly into the spot she had just vacated. Chet was very impressed by the maneuver, and I told him that it was really nothing because I'd driven a cab in Portland, Maine for seven years, in all kinds of weather, and got used to pulling in and out of very tight parking places.

The two of us got out and made our way over to a big, lush, grassy area shaded by palm trees overlooking the vast expanse of ocean. Chet said he really liked the spot I chose and said Bird would have dug it there also.

We walked a little further until we came to a small quiet area at the very edge of the cliff where it overlooked the roadway, which ran along the coastline of Santa Monica Beach. Here we had an unimpeded view across the ocean to the horizon. Chet seemed to really feel at ease here and quickly sat down on the grass. I followed suit. We lit up cigarettes and sort of fell into a loose conversation. He started talking about his early career and playing with Charlie Parker. I noticed that when he spoke of Charlie Parker, sadness would fill his face and he'd get silent and pensive.

I studied him for a while, then turned and looked out over the ocean, reflecting on my years as a sailor aboard the war ship USS Des Moines, and the time I first heard Chet over the radio. He had been playing *The Lamp is Low*. Now, here I was sitting right beside him on the grass at Santa Monica Beach. I was anxious to know more about Bird, especially from Chet's point of view - what it was like when he first met him, what it was like when he'd been chosen and hired to play with his group, what it must have been like to be on the road with Bird.

I had sat in with Charlie Parker before. When I was seventeen or so, I hitchhiked to New York City from Maine to see him at The Royal Roost and maybe get a chance to sit in with him and his band. I tried to convince the guy at the door I was eighteen. It didn't work. He sent me over to a bullpen-like area where they let underage kids sit and watch. At the end of his set Bird walked past and I got up the nerve to call out to him.

"Mr. Parker! Mr. Parker!" He stopped and turned to me.

"Who's that calling me Mr. Parker?"

I introduced myself and I asked if I could sit in with him and his group. He asked me what I played.

"I play drums, I think."

"What do you mean, 'you think'?" He was smiling, warm and gracious to this young kid who couldn't even be sure he was a drummer.

"I don't own a set of drums," I explained. "And I can't read music, so I dunno."

He looked over at the great Max Roach who was playing drums that night and the two of them smiled, then he told me to hang around until the last set and he'd see what he could do.

When the time came, Bird had me come up to the stand. The first tune was his composition, *Cheryl's Blues*, which was at a medium tempo. The second tune was faster, but I managed to hold it together. Afterward he told me I was a little raw, but I had great "time and rhythm and a natural sense of placement." He also told me to go home and do some "woodshedding" and look him up in a few months.

Now, at my house we had to carry wood from the cellar to the second floor for the kitchen stove and in my seventeen year old mind, I took Bird's words to heart and started lugging up wood to stack in the back hall. My father wondered at my intense activity. I told him that Charlie Parker told me I had to woodshed. That made my father laugh.

"Son, stacking wood is not what he means. He wants you to practice."

And that's what I did. Several months later, I again went to

New York, this time to Birdland. I got to sit in on several songs. "Now you're sweeping the store clean!" he told me. I didn't need that phrase translated – it was clear that Charlie Parker was pleased with my improvement.

That was a big moment for me as an aspiring musician, but I knew it couldn't compare to the sensation and thrill Chet must have felt when Charlie Parker chose him to play trumpet with him for several gigs on the West Coast. Chet must have been on cloud nine.

The world knew that Parker had a heroin addiction and I wondered if that had influenced Chet. I wasn't sure how he was going to take my next question, but it was something I felt I just had to know.

"Hey, Chet – did Bird ever try to get you to shoot up with him?" When he heard that, Chet's eyes narrowed and speared me with a real angry look.

"Bird never tried to lay any shit on me, man. Whenever I was with Bird, playing in different clubs, staying in different hotels, Bird would always keep an eye on the pushers, waiting for them to make their play. And when any one of them made a move toward me, he'd get real pissed off and put his body between mine and the pusher's, raise his fist and tell them not to fuck with me because I was off limits, then stand there eyeballing them until they'd leave."

Chet continued to talk about Bird with a sense of pride. "He protected me like I was his own son." I would come to learn over the succeeding days, weeks and months, that Chet loved to talk about Bird, and about times spent with him. I also learned that his stories were, more often than not, filled with bitter sweetness and pain.

Chet commenced to tell me things about Bird I hadn't known – that Bird had a lot of personal problems and more than one personality.

"Yeah," Chet continued, "he'd go through a whole lot of changes behind the shit, man. Copping, drinking two or three fifths of Hennessy a day…" He stopped talking and looked off past me for a few seconds, and when he turned back, I could see a glistening in his eyes.

"There'll never be another player like the Bird." He paused a moment, then sighed. "One of the great things I'll always remember about him was his kindness. He was one of the most giving cats I ever knew."

He held both of his hands out in front of him, about chest high, and began to examine them slowly. He turned them over and studied the palms for a few seconds, then reversed them and studied his knuckles and fingers. He looked at his hands and fingers for a couple of minutes.

"Something wrong with your hands, man?" I asked.

He raised his head while continuing to look at his hands. "Ohhhh... I was just thinking about how lucky I was that my hands and fingers weren't permanently damaged, too." He raised them up and studied them again.

"You mean when you were beaten up?"

"Yeah, it's one thing to lose your teeth... but, without hands and fingers..."

There was a distinct pain and sadness in his voice. I wanted Chet to know I was there for him, and I was interested in everything he had to say, no matter how long it happened to take.

"What is it, man? What's troubling you?"

He took another drag off the cigarette, then ground it out in the grass. He said he really didn't want to talk about anything at that time and just wanted to be alone in his thoughts for a few minutes. I told him I understood. I really didn't know how or what to say to him at a time like this and figured it best to be patient and wait for him to say something.

Minutes went by and he just continued to stare blankly out over the ocean. I started to really get concerned and decided to break through his wall of silence. Quietly, I asked again what it was that was troubling him so much. When he turned and looked at me, I could see tears welling up in his eyes. He tried his best to cover it. Finally he answered me in a soft whispery-like tone of voice.

"I'm concerned man, really concerned," he said. He rubbed his left forearm nervously. I knew he wasn't kidding. I could hear it in his voice and see the look of fear on his face. He then rubbed a hand across his eyes and nervously bit the inside of his lip. Finally, he got around to telling me what was eating away at him so much.

Chet had a real fear that he'd never be able to play the trumpet the same way again, if at all. He spoke of his deep concern that due to the severity of what he had gone through, the possibility of being unable to play and provide for his family could actually happen. Carol and his kids and playing trumpet were all he really cared about. They were his whole world, and nothing else mattered to him.

He was deeply troubled. I reached over and put my arm around his shoulder. I didn't know what to say or do at that moment. I had never faced anything so serious that could result in my never being able to play drums again. This was his whole life. Make no mistake about it. Chet could play, but it was nowhere near the same ability and strength he'd had before. I believe that's what troubled him the most.

I was grounded in a rock solid faith in God and I felt certain that Chet would get his chops back. I said this to him, telling him to have faith and trust that he would play again. He looked at me skeptically and managed a smile. I knew he wanted to believe me, but really didn't know quite what to say. I told him I prayed every day and night and knew for sure that my prayers were always heard and answered. I told him I believed he was going to be playing again one day soon and perhaps even better than he ever had. He looked at me, weighing over what I had said, while I wondered if I had offended him in any way. Finally, he broke the silence and smiled.

"Thanks, Art. I appreciate your faith, man," he said with quiet sincerity. "I want you to know that I really treasure your friendship. And really, I mean that, too, man."

He took in a deep breath and held it for a few seconds, then exhaled slowly, the last part of the breath sounding like a sigh of disgust.

"I thought I had a lot of friends, you know? Like all the cats I hired to do gigs with me and all the cats that recorded with me…" He stopped talking and sat there looking off, bewildered, for a few minutes or so. "Whenever I called one of them on the phone, before I even had the chance to ask for anything, each one of them had the same ready-made excuse. The 'I'd like to help you Chet, but…' kind of thing, you know? And it was pretty much the same way with the record producers, A & R men and club owners too. They didn't want a thing to do with me, man. Every one of those I thought were my friends…weren't."

I really felt bad for him, and sincerely hoped that in time he'd come to know that he had found a true friend, someone who was there to extend an open hand of kindness rather than the heel of a boot. I hoped to convince and inspire him to believe that what he once was, he could be again. I believed we had met for that purpose, for me to help bring him back into the limelight.

I was getting hungry and remembered passing a Winchell's Donuts shop on the way. I told Chet I wanted to get myself a coffee and a couple of doughnuts and asked if he wanted me to get him something.

"Yeah, if you don't mind, get me a couple of those powdered sugar jelly doughnuts… I really dig those."

When I got back Chet was still seated on the grass smoking a cigarette and toying with his shoelace. I sat down and handed him a cup of coffee and one of the powdered jelly doughnuts. Before I could even get my coffee cup up to my mouth, he had eaten half a jelly doughnut, and the next bite finished it off entirely. I finished mine and ate our second one, sitting there laughing at each other because our mouths were covered with white powder.

Still smiling, he took a couple sips of coffee and wiped the rest of the powdered sugar off his face, remarking how delicious the doughnuts were. I fully agreed. Chet became so deathly silent and I had a feeling it had to do with the fact I'd paid for the coffee and doughnuts and perhaps it had hurt his feelings. I asked him how he was fixed for bread. I explained that I wasn't trying to be nosey or anything like that but I wanted to help.

He looked at me with a curious frown. He related how he really hadn't been able to find steady work, and because of that… he abruptly stopped talking for a few seconds, then with reluctance, confessed that he and Carol had gone on welfare. It embarrassed and pissed him off, making him feel like he was a loser. After he told me that, he lowered his head between his legs and remained that way for minutes.

I felt this real sense of helplessness. I really wanted to help him, though I didn't have a lot of bread myself. I told him I could lay a few bucks on him until things started happening for him. He regarded me with this long pensive look and thanked me for my genuine concern, but he knew that I was really no better off than he was. I told him that may be the case, but there was a difference and that difference was the fact that I was working, and had a lot of house painting jobs ahead.

A thought hit me and I asked him if he'd like to work with me painting houses. I told him I was doing a house in Beverly Hills and if he came to work with me, he could start late in the morning and work as many hours as he wanted and I'd still give him decent bread. He quietly weighed the whole idea over. While he was mulling it over, I went on to tell him I'd be painting Nicky Blair's house the following week, and mentioned how Nicky had lined up a few famous movie star's homes for me to paint as soon as I'd finished his.

Chet wanted to know just who this Nicky Blair person was and how I had met him. I told him when Earla and I decided to move to L.A., I was told by my barber to make sure I looked up his cousin, Nicky Blair and close friend, Michael Dante, who was an actor. After Earla and I had settled our family into our little house in Culver City, I focused more on getting paint jobs to feed us and pay the bills, then I did anything or anyone one else. On some nights I'd go to the jazz clubs and sit in with musicians around town in order to keep my chops up. It wasn't until I happened to be watching a television show one night when I remembered that Michael Dante was starring on the television series "Custer" where he played the part of Crazy Horse. The very next day I called Michael on the set at the studio and surprisingly he answered. I told him who I was and asked if he could possibly get me a small part on his show. He was very apologetic and told me that this was the last day of shooting for the series. He said he'd be happy to meet me, and was sure that Nicky Blair would be as well. He gave me directions on how to get to Nicky's restaurant, and asked me to meet him there around 8 p.m. I was there on the dot.

Stefanino's Trattoria was a famous Italian restaurant on Sunset Boulevard in Beverly Hills. It was frequented by the major names of show business, including Frank Sinatra, who would eat there two or three times a week when he was in town. I was introduced to Frank by Nicky as his cousin, and thereafter, every time I'd see Frank in the restaurant, he'd ask how I was doing. I nearly wound up getting a part in one of his movies, *Robin and the Seven Hoods,* but unfortunately, the part had already been cast.

Whenever I was at Nicky's house he'd get a ton of phone calls. He had three different lines and often Nicky would have me answer one of the phones when he was talking on another line. He'd also get a lot of mail. The one thing I remember most of all was how Frank Sinatra signed his letters to Nicky. He'd write, "Love and Spaghetti." Frank was unique.

Stefanino's interior had old Italian stucco walls with brick coming through, dark stained beams and plush red leather booths in two rooms and a medium/long and very busy bar. I immediately recognized Michael, who was at least 6' 4" standing with a shorter man, who turned out to be Nicky Blair, who was the manager and part owner of the restaurant. The three of us went into another section of the place and grabbed a booth. We talked for almost an hour and hit it off well. I told them I was a jazz drummer and also a top-notch house painter. Michael and Nicky owned several bungalows in Westwood and wanted to know if I'd be interested in doing some painting for them. I was, and started the very next day. We soon became good friends.

I told Chet that everybody in show business gathered at the place – big name producers, directors, screenwriters, actors and actresses and just about every other kind of famous person frequented this restaurant on a regular basis. It was the place to be seen and to dine on the great, award-winning Italian cuisine.

"And dig this, Chet," I went on. "Nicky's partner is Steve Crane, Lana Turner's ex-husband. Do you know who I'm talking about?"

"Yeah… is he the same cat who owns restaurants all around L.A.?"

"Yeah, and all over the world, too. Anyway, Steve's a great cat and I'm going to be doing some painting for him pretty soon, also. And dig this, Chet, I can go to Stefanino's any night of the week and eat any dish I want to and it never costs me a cent. So, if you work with me, Nicky would probably let you do the same thing. Maybe even invite you to bring Carol up to eat a couple times a week, you know? So what do you think, man, you interested?"

I noticed that whenever something pleased Chet he'd smile and open his eyes wide like he wanted the whole world to enter in. Chet still had this little boy quality inside his heart.

He told me he really needed the bread and was willing to work his ass off to earn it, and would be ready to start the following Monday. I told him I'd pick him up at his house on Monday morning. But he didn't want me to have to do that because it was too far for me to come. He'd borrow his mother's car and meet me at my house. I learned another thing about Chet right there, and that was he was also very considerate. To say I was happy that Chet and I were going to be working together on a job or two would be an understatement.

Chapter 9
Going Down Memory Lane

Chet stretched, looked out over the ocean, and went on to tell me about his childhood in Yale, Oklahoma and how poor they had been because his dad couldn't find work in town. Eventually, they had to go live with his mother's parents in Oklahoma City.

He smiled when he mentioned his grandparents – the fun he'd had going into their garden, grabbing a big, fat watermelon, running back behind the red barn and dropping it on the ground. It would split in two and he would just sit down and happily eat the juicy red heart out of it. When he spoke of these moments in his childhood, his face beamed with joy. But when he spoke of other moments, especially about his mother and father and their bickering over him, his facial muscles tightened.

When they lived in Oklahoma City, his dad played banjo in a hotel there. At times, he'd come home drunk and ornery. This always upset his mother and made Chet unhappy, angry, disgusted and ashamed. When I asked him why he thought his father drank so much and why he was always so angry, Chet let out this long painful sigh and frowned. His mother told him that his father didn't have the extra gift of talent that Chet had, and because of that, he'd be angry and disappointed and sit around the house feeling sorry for himself and drowning his troubles in beer.

It was easy to see on his face that this obviously bothered Chet a lot.

"I don't know if I could've handled something like that from my dad," I said quietly.

"He was okay, I guess," he said, and shrugged. "The times were just pretty hard then, you know?" It came across to me that Chet was trying to convince himself to feel sorry for his dad.

I asked Chet if his dad was a mean kind of man. Would he beat him if Chet did something his father didn't approve of? He said no, his dad had never really beaten him as such, but there had been an incident or two, like this one time when they were living at his grandparent's farm in Oklahoma. He told me about how his dad had become pissed at him because he hadn't gotten up early enough to chop wood for the kitchen stove, and because of it, the fire had gone out. His father definitely let him know about it.

"I walked into the kitchen and the next thing I felt was a hand hitting me on the back and my knees hitting the floor, and when I looked up, there was my father standing over me looking down at me." He smiled painfully as he remembered. "There may have been another time too a little bit later on," he said, and let that thought die.

Apparently, Chet's mother heard his father yelling at him and came rushing into the kitchen to see what the commotion was all about. When she saw 'Chetty,' as she always called him, standing in a corner facing the wall, she rushed to him and started gushing and fussing over him as she always did. He said, her treating him like that always tended to make him feel inferior and it would give him a feeling of disgust.

"I hated it whenever she'd coddle me and treat me like a baby in front of my father or my friends. It's no wonder my father got pissed off at her. I was the center of her world. She'd sign me up for talent shows, having me sing these romantic ballads. And most of the time, she made it seem like my father was nothing more than a secondary fixture around the house. That bothered me, you know? But there was nothing I could do about it."

His mother, Vera, was convinced that Chet was a singing prodigy.

"My mother was constantly fussing over me and rushing me to every talent contest she could find. And she always entered me as a singer, hoping I'd win first prize. But I never would because they'd always give the prize to some dancer or to some fat accordion player. And that made me happy because I figured she'd finally get discouraged, and stop taking me to other talent contests," he said and sighed deeply. "But she didn't."

"Was your father a big man physically?" I asked.

"Well, he really wasn't a big man as such. He was maybe 5 feet, 11 inches, had a medium build, but," he stopped a moment, then added with child-like pride, "He had some pretty good-sized muscles in his arms. I guess that came from working in the plane factory, and playing banjo. That's all I ever heard him do was play that banjo. He was a damn good player, too."

I sensed that even though his dad had some inner jealousy of his son, Chet nonetheless really liked his father a lot. But it seemed he was pretty much unable to express it due to his mother's constant coddling and excessive favoring of her Chetty over her own husband.

Chet talked about how it had really bothered his father a lot that he wasn't able to earn enough money playing the banjo to put food on the table. His father said if they didn't hurry up and leave Oklahoma soon, they'd all starve and have to go to the poor house.

I knew exactly what he was talking about because it had been pretty much the same for my dad and mom and my other brothers and sisters growing up in the Depression years in Maine.

Chet told me that a couple of days after his parents' conversation about the poor house, his dad took off in his car and drove to Los Angeles, found and rented a small house, landed a job at an airplane factory in Glendale and then sent for Chet and his mother. He and his mother didn't have the money to fly out, so they had to take the bus. The bus ride, he told me, was a 'fucking drag,' and how beat the two of them were by the time they pulled into the bus terminal in Los Angeles. And yet, the very next day his mother went to work for W.T. Grant downtown. Within a week, he said, she'd started all over again with the same talent show bullshit.

When he told me about the talent show thing, I couldn't help myself and started to laugh. Chet looked at me sternly with those deep-set eyes. I thought he was really pissed at me for laughing. But then, ever so slowly, the stern look gave way and his face illuminated into this big warm smile.

"My mother would go to the 'Five and Dime' store and buy every song sheet that was popular, and come home and have me learn the melodies and lyrics to every one of them."

That pretty much explained why he knew so damn many

tunes. I thought to myself, man, he was singing all those beautiful romantic love songs when he was only ten years old. When I mentioned this to him he looked at me and smiled that humble boyish smile, the smile that was solely Chet's. He had a way of looking at you that could make you feel warm and wanted, or small and unnecessary. I was really interested in knowing how he'd learned to sing and play all those tunes. To say the least, it was a bit uncanny.

Chet also explained that when he didn't feel like learning new songs his mother would go to the bakery and bring home white powdered jelly doughnuts and bribe him, telling him that for each new song he'd learn, she'd give him a big fat powdered sugar jelly doughnut. He laughed reflectively and said he learned all those songs because he couldn't help himself. He dug eating the powdered jelly doughnuts too much. This was something else I'd learned about Chet – he really loved sweets.

All of the singing really pissed his father off royally because it was his feeling that Chet's mother was turning their son into a little weakling by always having Chet sing songs.

Chet said his father strongly impressed upon his mother that he wanted his son to grow up to be a man, and that he should be doing other things instead of eating jelly doughnuts and singing songs. She quickly reminded him that he was also her son.

"All my father wanted was for me to do more of the chores around the house and to learn how to play some kind of instrument," Chet said. His parents would have arguments about it from time to time, and he always felt, on this point, his father was right about his learning to do other things.

"I really believe she knew it too, but she'd never admit it to him. Anyway, I started doing all the chores around the house and that made my father happy and took a lot of pressure off of me… at least until this one morning when my father caught me playing his prized banjo. Man, he grabbed that banjo out of my hands and was about to kick the shit out of me when my mother came into the room and jumped all over him. She told him that just because he had lost his job playing banjo at the hotel, it didn't give him the right to take it out on me and treat me like a dog."

"Did he ever really kick the shit out of you, you know, hurt you bad or anything?"

"No… he never did, although, there was this one time…" he stopped and thought about something, then continued. "He'd been drinking a lot and told me in no uncertain terms to keep my hands off of his frigging banjo. Then he yelled at my mother and told her that I needed to be disciplined and she hadn't done too good a job of doing that."

Listening to Chet talk was great. According to what Carol had said to me, Chet rarely, if ever, talked to anybody about himself, especially about his childhood. Yet, here he was, completely relaxed, and talking to me about his time as a kid with the ease of sparks flying up from an open fire.

"I never touched his banjo again… at least not when I had the feeling he might be in the vicinity, you know?"

Chet went on about how his father had come home one night with a trombone in his hand and gave it to him and told him to learn how to play it instead of doing all that singing shit his mother was having him do. He told Chet that he'd probably be able to get a job in some band if he learned how to master the thing.

"I took the trombone into my bedroom and tried to play it but couldn't because my arms weren't long enough to control the slide, no matter how hard I tried."

"So what did you do with the 'bone?"

"Well… I didn't want to piss my father off or hurt his feelings… so I just kept on trying to play. And the harder I tried the more frustrated I got. I just couldn't handle that damn slide…."

The longer we talked the better I got to know him. And one of the most important things I was coming to learn about Chet Baker was the unmistakable fact that he had an extremely strong will and also, this kind of a 'I'm not going to give up' inner strength kind of thing. He amazed me, he really did. He'd had it all and now he'd been reduced to a common man, and yet, he still had this driving flame burning within.

I asked if he learned to master the trombone or if he had given it back to his dad. He started telling me about this one night when he was still a kid and his father had three of his musician friends over to the house to play cards in the kitchen. He said they were drinking beer and smoking marijuana.

"Well, I was in my bedroom trying to play that damn trombone and heard one of the men in the kitchen start laughing and ask my father if he had a wounded elephant in the next room or something? And all the other men started laughing, including my father."

His father told his cronies that he had bought the trombone to keep his kid occupied and out of trouble. One of them laughed again and asked why he hadn't bought his son a guitar, saying that it would have been a hell of a lot easier on their ears if he had. He said his father told them that the boy wanted to play a horn so he got him a horn.

"Did what those guys say bother you, or hurt your feelings, Chet?"

"No…no, it didn't bother me in the least, man, because I really didn't care for the sound of the trombone anyway. What I had really wanted was something a little lighter… something that I could handle."

"Did you tell your father how you felt about it, or mention it to your mother?"

He related how he had gone into the living room that night where his mother was sitting by herself, and told her that he couldn't play the trombone because it was just too big for him to handle. He said all she did was smile and tell him that maybe he should forget all about playing a horn and just stick to his singing.

He got real pissed and told her that he wanted to play a horn, but one that he could handle. She promised she'd speak to his father the next day about getting him a trumpet, and asked if that made him happy. He told her it did and that he'd be able to master the trumpet much easier. She assured him that she'd take the matter up with his father in the morning.

But in the meantime, she informed him that it was past his bedtime. As he crossed to his bedroom, his nostrils suddenly became filled with what he described as a strange woody kind of tobacco smell that caused him to cough and choke. Chet said he went back to his mother and asked what she thought the smell might be. She made light of it, telling him it was probably some new kind of pipe tobacco or something and that he should forget about it and just get to sleep.

Chet went to bed, but couldn't sleep. A little while later, he heard his mother jumping all over his father for smoking marijuana in their house with his drunken cronies. She told his father in no uncertain terms that it wasn't right for him and his friends to be sitting around the house drinking, laughing and poking fun at his own son like they had. His father blew up and told her that if she didn't like it, it was tough shit, and that he was sick and tired of her not ever leaving Chet alone to try to do some of the things he might want to do instead of always having to do the things she wanted him to do. Chet said it just seemed to him that his mother held a resentment against his father because, as she saw it, his father wasn't spending enough time with his boy, and that if he had any sense, he'd want to show his only son how to do things instead of sitting around the house with his crazy musician friends.

"Man, she really lit into him about smoking pot in the house with his friends. I remember it like it was yesterday," he said, a light smile on his face. "She told my father that she hoped I would never take up smoking that nasty marijuana."

He stopped and lowered his head for a couple seconds, and when he looked up at me, he had a look on his face like he was ashamed that he had ever started smoking it himself.

"I knew they were going to continue arguing so I got up out of bed and went outside and just sat there thinking about what I could do to help them get along with each other better…"

I lit up a cigarette and offered one to Chet. He took a long drag, exhaling slowly, and continued to talk about his parents. Though his mother was soft spoken and introspective, and his father could be mean and ornery when he was drinking, Vera wasn't afraid to stand up to him, and his dad knew it, too. She'd criticize him for drinking and tell him he was setting a bad example for his son. And that if he really cared for his son like he said he did, then he'd want to do all he could to make his son happy, like taking the big trombone back and getting him something he could handle, like a trumpet.

"How'd your father take that, was he pissed at her?"

"Well, not really… he just told her that he'd see what he could do about exchanging the trombone for a trumpet the next day, and that was it."

His father had recently taken a part time job and wouldn't get home until after suppertime. I saw the burning excitement on Chet's face as he relived those moments from years past, his being young and really wanting and hoping that his dad would bring him home a trumpet.

"Man," he said reflecting. "After school that day I waited in the kitchen for my father to get home from work just to see if he had really brought me home a trumpet or not. Finally, about 7:30 that night, he came in through the kitchen door and he was holding one hand behind his back. He came right over to me and knelt down and told me that he had a surprise for me, and then he placed the trumpet into my hands."

His eyes glistened for a while. He told me he made a promise to his father that he would learn to play the trumpet so good that he'd make his father very proud of him.

"Man, you sure made that promise come true, and then some!"

"Well, I guess," he said with complete modesty. "I soon found out that I was able to play just about anything I heard over the radio or on records and my father was amazed by that."

Chet noticed it was getting late in the afternoon. We were both amazed at where all the time had gone. "Carol's probably wondering where we are about now, so we'd better make it out of here," he said and got up off the grass and brushed himself off. While we made our way over to the car, all he talked about was his concern for Carol and she'd be worried about him.

That told me a lot about the man, Chet Baker. It showed he had a genuine concern and thoughtfulness for his wife's personal cares and concerns. And I felt it was quite remarkable for a man who had this reputation of being nothing more than a selfish drug addict who cared only for his own needs, yet, here he was, concerned about not wanting to worry his wife. To me, that said a whole lot about Chet's heart.

There is a leisurely, but fairly quick way to Redondo Beach from Santa Monica, up over La Brea into Inglewood and on to the freeway. This day, I took the long way because I was absorbing everything Chet had said. We got to Redondo Beach and it was starting to get dark.

Suddenly, an on-coming car was coming straight at us, causing me to immediately swerve the car off the side of the road and into a gravel covered driveway. We came to an abrupt stop about four inches from crashing into a small real estate office building. I breathed a thankful sigh of relief realizing we had just missed possible death, or at the least, some permanent type of injury.

I figured it had to have been my fault because I wasn't concentrating on the road ahead. My first concern was for Chet. Was he all right? Had he been injured? I asked with genuine concern. Chet quietly assured me he was perfectly all right. He seemed totally unaffected by what had just transpired, and then, with no more excitement than that of tossing a cigarette out of the window, he looked around and recognized where my car had come to a stop. He gestured up ahead and asked if I'd mind pulling up to the small variety store some 100 feet away.

I couldn't really believe it. He was just so casual about it all. I told him I didn't mind, straightened myself out and pulled the car up to the front of the variety store and parked. I was still a little shocked about nearly being involved in an accident, but was much more shocked by the next thing I heard come out of Chet's mouth.

Chapter 10
A Dime For a Bunch of Carrots

"You got a dime, Art? Carol's making a stew and she wanted me to pick up a bunch of carrots," he said in a matter-of-fact tone.

We'd just barely missed being injured in a car wreck and here was my all-time inspiration in all of jazz, asking me for such a little sum of money so that he could buy a bunch of carrots for his wife to make a stew. I wondered if I had somehow misunderstood what he'd asked me. But that was all. I saw in that one gesture, a man that few, if any, had ever had the opportunity to see. Here was a man who had soared to the top of the music world, and here he was now, a husband like any other husband, remembering to bring his wife a simple ingredient for dinner. This was the same man who had so oftentimes been maligned by writers and critics, people who knew nothing about the personal side of Chet Baker.

I went into the variety store with him to look around. Chet went immediately to the produce bin at the rear of the store and grabbed a bunch of carrots. I asked if that was all he needed. He slowly looked around and asked in a soft-spoken tone if I had enough money to buy something else for him without having to go without myself. I had about 25 bucks on me, more than enough to buy him whatever else he may have needed.

"Sure, what else do you want, Chet?"

"Well…I'd like to get a couple packs of Pall Mall cigarettes."

"No problem. You need anything else?"

He smiled and shook his head. "No, that's all I need, man."

When we got to the small, one-aisle checkout area, Chet placed the carrots on the counter and asked the cashier to get him the cigarettes. It came to little more than a buck and change. Not wanting to embarrass Chet, I quickly reached into my pocket and took out a 20 dollar bill and slipped it into his hand. Chet handed the twenty to the cashier. After he rang it up the cashier handed Chet the change and we left the store. Chet gave the rest of the change back, thanked me, and told me that he would never forget my kindness. I tried to give him a ten spot but he waved it away, saying he'd be all right. I started the car and headed for Redondo Beach. Although I said nothing, I felt sorrow for Chet's situation.

When I pulled up to his house, the front door opened. The silhouetted figure of Carol stood in a square of light emanating from the living room behind her. She called out and invited me in. Chet likewise asked me to come in for a while, so I did.

The three kids, Dean, Paul and little Missy were seated on the couch intently watching cartoons on a small television set. Carol greeted me with a warm smile and began preparing the stew. Chet excused himself and left Carol and I at the kitchen table.

I started to tell Carol how I felt I was gaining Chet's trust. She looked me straight in the eye and told me that it wasn't going to be an easy thing to do. She spoke of how there had been so many people who wanted a piece of Chet; how they had made many promises in order to get on the good side of him and then none of those promises had ever come through. Chet, she went on to say, trusted no one, because as soon as they knew he could no longer play, they turned their backs on him.

I let her know this didn't surprise me because something similar had also happened to me, though nowhere near the importance of what happened to Chet. When I mentioned how much Chet had already revealed of himself to me, she seemed surprised. A wistful smile broke out over her beautiful face. I got the distinct feeling she knew I was really there to help Chet, rather than for what I could get from his being a big name.

Chet rejoined us at the table as Carol got up to make a pot of tea. She asked me to stay for dinner and Chet quickly seconded her invitation. I thanked her for inviting me, but I had to get back home, because Earla and I had already made other plans.

On the way home, my mind was a rainstorm of activity. Carol's invitation to stay for dinner meant a lot to me. It was an important gesture on her part and I could feel her growing trust. I thought that would go a long way in building a solid friendship between Chet and me.

I also thought about how life can play out in ways you could have never planned. Although I had prayed that I would someday meet Chet Baker and play onstage with him. I never expected to become his friend, or get to know his family.

The main reason I had brought my family out to Los Angeles was to build a career in acting. My hope and dream, like so many before and so many since, was to come to Hollywood, and try to make it in movies. My goal was to make enough money as an actor so my father wouldn't have to work seven days a week in a dark, dank and damp mill anymore. He'd had severe emphysema, chronic bronchitis and asthma, and wound up dying of pneumonia on his only week of vacation at the age of 57. I had come nowhere close to that goal. When my father died, I had 11 cents in my pocket... a dime and a penny. Still, I decided I wasn't going to give up on my dream of achieving something in acting or music. I ran an acting class out of my house. I had been a stage actor and had done several plays. Hopefully a break would come, and I'd be cast in a good supporting role, and have the chance to buy my mother the little red brick house she liked so much. I continued to make the rounds to all the major studios, meeting casting directors and a couple producers. But that didn't happen either.

It was a funny thing. On the one hand, I truly believed I could have gotten a lot of good roles in movies. I thought I really wanted success. But on the other hand, I was afraid of what success often brought with it. I'd seen what it had done to others and acting became more of a professional hobby than a career. I went back to my first love, playing jazz drums. And as soon as I did, I was playing and sitting in with most of the major name musicians around the greater Los Angeles area. And it was the decision to return to music that I firmly believe God led me to Donte's jazz club in North Hollywood and my re-union with Chet.

Now, the only thing on my mind was to get Chet back to the top where he so rightfully belonged. I prayed for guidance on how to help this great musician play the music he loved so dearly and remain steady in his success.

My thoughts on that drive home brought me a lot of clarity.

When I pulled into my yard, my three kids were outside playing and were happy to see me. They'd been waiting for me to get home so we could play Monopoly. This kind of homecoming was the success that kept me steady.

In the coming weeks of our growing friendship, Chet, who still didn't have a phone, would sometimes call from one of his neighbors. He would ask if I could drive him to his mother's workplace so he could borrow her car, or sometimes he just wanted to get out of the house for a while. This one time, when he called, I had some free time. I wasn't on a job painting, and Earla didn't need me for anything that day, so I headed to Redondo Beach.

When I got there he invited me to come inside to meet his mother, Vera. She was a pretty lady and spoke slowly and softly, and like Chet, had that same Oklahoma drawl. Though Chet did resemble his late father some, to me he was the spitting image of his mother. She seemed very interested in me, and what I did, and I felt she had a concern – a hope if you will – that I would be a loyal friend to her son.

Chet was impatient about leaving. He grabbed one of his record albums, one that featured a full-face shot of him, and made his way to the door with me close behind him.

"You'd better not forget to put your sweater on, Chetty, because it might get cold later in the day," his mother called out.

Chet had this look of disgust and frustration over his face. Carol gave me the proverbial 'What can I say' type of look.

"I'll be fine. I don't need a sweater," Chet responded and quickly walked out the door. I then understood his impatience.

In the car, Chet went on about how much it bothered him when his mother treated him like he was still a kid. I told him my mother at times still treated me the same way – it was probably just a mother's way of showing us that even though we were grown men, that we'd always be a kid in their eyes.

I asked him where he wanted me to take him and he said, South Central. He assured me that everything would be, as he'd often put it, 'cool.'

I didn't like the idea. I quickly let him know that even though I thought the world of him, respected and trusted him completely, there was just NO way I was going anywhere near that barber shop again if I could help it.

He laughed, and said, "No, it's a whole different place, Art."

Chapter 11
Back to Watts

I knew what he was there for this time. He asked me to drive down this one particular street, which was in the opposite direction of the barbershop and had me stop a few feet away from this small pale yellow house. He turned and looked over his shoulders, then up and down the street a couple of times until he felt sure there were no cops in the area. Satisfied, he grabbed the album and said he'd be back in a short while, got out and walked hurriedly across the street to the rear door of the house and knocked a few times. I didn't take my eyes off of him for a second because I wanted to make certain nothing happened to him.

There was no answer at first so he knocked again. Still, no answer. He turned and glanced over at me, and just as he did, a big black man opened the door. Chet immediately turned around to greet him. The man obviously didn't know or recognize him, so Chet held up the album. The man smiled and let Chet in, closing the door behind him.

I lit up a cigarette and turned on the radio and listened to KBCA-FM, a jazz radio station in L.A., and believe it or not, they were actually playing one of Chet's records. I'll never forget that, or the tune they were playing. It was a beautifully haunting ballad called, *Lush Life*. Hearing that sent shivers up and down my spine.

After the tune ended, the DJ announced the musicians accompanying Chet – Russ Freeman on piano, Leroy Vinegar on bass and Shelly Manne on drums. Listening to Chet play was what it must be like to listen to the archangel, Gabriel. Chet's tone was so pure, so round and so warm. I had never heard any other trumpet player play quite the same way. It was incredible! And now, tragically, Chet was no longer able to play that way. I couldn't begin to imagine his anguish.

While waiting for Chet to come back, my eyes focused on the intersection up ahead for signs of black 'n' whites suddenly appearing, or unmarked cars with the letter 'E' on their license plates. Many cars drove by, but I didn't see any police cars. Then I saw Chet coming out of the yellow house, slowly making his way over to the car. Reaching it, he opened the door and slid his weary body into the front seat, leaned his head back against the headrest and closed his eyes. He'd left the car door wide open. I got out, shut the door, got back behind the wheel, and quickly drove away. I didn't want to hang around the area in the event a police car just happened to drive by and spot me, so I drove a few blocks and pulled into the lot of a big grocery store and parked at the far end.

I looked down at Chet and noticed that his breathing was quite shallow and that scared me. I spoke to him and within ten or fifteen seconds he responded, although wearily. But his response was a hell of a lot faster than it had been from the time I'd taken him to that fucked-up barbershop. He opened his eyes, and without moving his head, looked around, then over to me and said that everything was cool and all right. It seemed the stuff he got this time had to have been a lot weaker than the 'soup shit' he got before. For that, I was very thankful. He closed his eyes again. A long sigh escaped from his mouth, and he drifted into sleep. I decided to take him back to Santa Monica Beach before heading home.

I found a beautiful spot close to where we had been before. We could look out over the seemingly endless ocean, or turn around and see a lovely section of downtown Santa Monica. I sat there quietly watching him, wondering why he had this need to take that heroin shit. I lit up a cigarette, took a few drags and decided to ask him then and there. I knew I'd be taking a gamble because he could say one of two things – tell me to mind my own damn business or, that he didn't want to talk about it.

I thought about it for a few minutes and decided it would be worth the risk for me to try and find out. I had begun to really care about him and wanted to get a deeper understanding of his need to use dope every day.

Taking a deep breath, I told him I realized I hadn't known

him long enough to ask him what I was about to ask, and I hoped he wouldn't get pissed at me for wanting to know, then I just stopped cold in my tracks. He looked at me curiously and asked what it was I wanted to know.

I thought, to hell with it, just come right out and ask him. And then the questions started coming one after the other. Why did he feel the need to take dope? Why did he ever get started on the shit in the first place? When did it all begin? I told him that I just couldn't understand it.

He put his hand on the side of his face and began to rub his cheek. Much to my surprise, he wasn't angry with me at all. Instead, he was very quiet and calm. After a while, he told me how it all started.

He hadn't had his first cigarette until he was 27 years old. I thought that was a little far-fetched, but didn't challenge him on it. He went on to say he'd first tried pot in late '52, early '53, when he was playing with Gerry Mulligan at the Haig, a small jazz club in Hollywood, off Wilshire Boulevard. Just about every musician he knew was smoking pot at the time.

"We had just finished playing a set and Gerry wanted to go out into the alley to get a breath of fresh air and have a smoke."

"Pot?" I inquired.

"No, he just had a cigarette. I didn't smoke at the time," he said. "I had been standing next to Gerry waiting for him to finish when this white cat dressed in a dark business suit walked up and pulled Gerry to one side and sold him some pot. Then he came back to me and wanted to sell me some, trying to convince me that it would make me feel good, loosen me up and help me to play even better. I told the cat that I was cool and didn't need any of that shit to make me feel good or play better. But this guy wouldn't give up, man… he went on about how all the other musicians were using it, and that it was the reason why they were all playing so free."

Chet said he thanked the guy and reaffirmed that he didn't want any, but the guy slipped some into his pocket anyway and told him to try it later. There was no charge, and if Chet didn't dig it, it would be all right. But if Chet did, then the man would be easy to find. The guy walked off whistling a tuneless tune, and Gerry stood by, laughing his ass off.

"Did you wind up smoking the pot that night, or did you throw it away?"

"No, I didn't throw it away. I actually waited 'til after the gig and lit it up in my car," he said. "At first, it made me light headed. Then after a while, I started laughing to myself for no reason, and couldn't stop. I thought, man, this shit really is great," he said and laughed.

I thought it hard to believe that had been the first time he'd ever smoked pot, but that's what he said, and I had no reason to doubt him.

Chet looked off for a few seconds and then quietly said how strange he thought it all was. "What do you mean, strange, Chet?"

"Life, it's all so strange…you know…."

"How do you mean?"

"Well…I've pretty much always believed I was put on earth for one reason, and that was to play trumpet."

I really didn't understand why he felt that way, or how he had come to such a conclusion. I knew that God had created us and put us on earth for far much more than to just play trumpet, drums, piano or whatever. That He had placed us here for higher reasons and purposes, which I tried to expound upon.

"Don't you believe God also put you on earth for other important things, like falling in love, getting married and having children?"

"Well, I'm not really sure I believe in God as such, Art. I just feel my playing is a spiritual thing, you know? That I was just put on earth to play trumpet for a while and then--" He didn't complete the sentence and that made me all the more curious.

"Then what?! What do you mean by THEN, Chet?" I asked.

He looked off again for a few moments but didn't say anything more. It was frustrating not getting a straight answer from him.

"Listen, man! I'm not trying to preach to you or anything like that, Chet, but if you're not sure about God, who IS Spirit, how can you say that being here on earth is a spiritual thing?"

He still didn't answer, so I kept going, trying to get through to him.

"If you really believe that you were only put on earth to play, and feel it's a spiritual thing, then why and where did your need to use dope come from? It doesn't make any sense at all, Chet."

He didn't say a word. Instead, he gave me this real icy stare, and I thought for sure he was going to get up and tell me to go straight to hell and never bother him again. But he didn't. Instead, he just sat there, silent. Then he lowered his head onto his knees. When he did look at me again, the pain in his eyes was clear.

I reasoned with him with compassion and reminded him that God had blessed him with many gifts. That he'd had it all. He had achieved worldwide fame, and still had a multitude of fans. Charlie Parker had always watched over him like he was his own son, never wanting Chet to even try dope, yet he did. I really wanted Chet to know how much his taking dope deeply troubled me. He finally looked up at me and managed a weak smile. I felt he was ready to talk.

"How'd you ever get started on heroin, especially after all the warnings you said Bird gave you about taking it? Why'd you do it, man? What made you start?"

He lit up a cigarette, looked straight into my eyes for a second or so, took a long drag and exhaled several smoke rings, and put his finger into each one of them until they vanished. Finally, he confessed that he started to take heroin purely out of curiosity.

After the sudden and untimely death of his friend, jazz pianist, Dick Twardzik, of a heroin overdose while they were on tour in Paris, Chet had come back to Los Angeles with a heavy heart and a ton of curiosity as to the why's and reasons of it all. He was sad over the loss of two good friends to heroin overdoses, and wanted to know exactly what there was in heroin that could, as he put it, "fuck up a person's mind and body enough to cause death." It was something he just had to figure out.

A while later, Chet was playing a gig in the L.A. area and ran into a musician friend who inquired about Twardzik's untimely demise, and wanted to know how it had happened. Chet said he told the guy all about it and how he had found it hard to understand why anyone in their right mind would ever want to take that kind of shit.

He said the musician told him not to knock it until he'd tried it for himself. He told Chet he had a 'balloon,' a packet of heroin, at his apartment and wanted to know if Chet was curious enough to learn about its effects. If so, Chet could accompany him to his apartment.

Chet said he knew the musician and had played with him before and felt he could trust him, so he accompanied him to his apartment. Once there, Chet related that the man went into the bathroom for several minutes, and then called Chet in to join him.

When he got in there, the man had drug paraphernalia spread out on a hamper, and was holding a burning match under a spoon cooking the stuff. When he finished, he took a syringe and needle and drew the hot liquid into it and asked Chet if he was still curious enough to want to try it. Chet told him he was, but wanted to 'skin pop' it first – inject it into the muscle first rather than the vein – so he wouldn't get hooked. The guy shot the shit into his deltoid muscle and he waited for a reaction, but got none. He said he tried it again a couple days later, but this time he shot directly into his vein. He got a real buzz, and liked it. Then he shot into his vein the following day, and the day after that, and knew he was hooked.

There was a long silence, and then a smile broke over his face. He looked into my eyes again and shrugged.

"Well," he said after a long, weary sigh, "I found out what heroin was all about, man."

He gave me another wry smile and left it at that. I didn't know what to say or think, so I didn't say a word. Instead, I said a silent prayer for him.

Chapter 12
The Road Back

On the drive to Redondo Beach, I asked Chet if he still had his flugelhorn. He lowered his head for a moment, then looked at me embarrassed. He'd had to hock it a few days before in order to put food on the table and didn't have the bread to get the horn back. I told him I'd buy it back for him if he made me a promise that once he had it, he'd practice until he was able to play again. He thought it over, then gave me his word he would. I told him I'd come by the next day to pick him up so the two of us could go get his horn.

The following day we drove to a street in Watts to a two-story house. Chet pointed to the upstairs door.

"Cat lives up there," he said and opened up his door. "The cat's a bad dude, so you better come with me," he said.

I told him to stay in the car and that I'd go up and take care of it for him. That was the boxer in me talking.

"He's a bad ass, so don't fuck with him," Chet warned. "Just give'im the bread, get the horn and get outta there."

"I gotcha, man. I'll be cool!" I said and made my way up the stairs and knocked on the door. There was no answer, so I knocked again. Within a few seconds, the door opened and there stood this big 6 foot 3 or 4 inch black dude standing in the frame. He sized me up and wanted to know what I was doing there and what I wanted. I told him who I was and that I was there to buy back Chet's flugelhorn. I reached into my pants pocket and pulled out a fifty-dollar bill. He smirked and said the price had gone up.

"What are you talking about?" I asked, surprised. "Chet told me it was fifty bucks."

"It was," he answered roughly, "but now it's a hundred bucks." He claimed the extra fifty was for safekeeping and storage fees. I got more than a little pissed and told him what he was doing was not right, that Chet had needed the money to buy food for his family, which had been his reason for pawning the horn in the first place, and that I was also just a working man with three kids who wanted to help Chet. The man just stood there straight-faced and uncaring. All he was interested in was getting the money.

"You want the horn back, man? Then come up with the extra bread!" he said gruffly. He went on to say that if I couldn't, then I should stop wasting his time and take a powder. I felt my anger rising and wanted to tell him to go fuck himself and that he was nothing but a cheap prick. But I knew I was beat and decided to give him the extra money. I pulled out the fifty and was about to give it to him but decided to make him bring the horn out to me before I did. He stepped back inside, brought the horn out and we made a quick exchange. Before I could say another word, the man shut the door in my face and left me standing there.

"What an arrogant bastard!" I said. I then lifted the horn up to look it over and make sure it was Chet's and make sure there were no dents and the like. Everything looked all right. I saw the Bach brand name and knew it was Chet's.

Excited to have it in my possession, I ran down over the stairs, taking them two at a time until I got to my car. But Chet was gone. I looked up and down the street, walked to the corner, looked up and down that street, still no sign of Chet. I couldn't figure out why he would want to leave knowing I was getting his horn back for him. Where would he go? Then it hit me like a Joe Louis right.

"He's going to see Leroy," I said aloud. I jumped into my car, slammed the key into the ignition and peeled out of there like a bat out of hell.

I didn't really know my way around the area so I drove around until I spotted the Watts Towers and knew I was close to the boulevard where Leroy's place was located. I found the street and hit the gas pedal, passing cars until I spotted the barbershop about a hundred feet ahead. And there was Chet walking toward it.

I blew the car horn, hoping to get Chet's attention, but to no avail. I was very nervous and scared that I wasn't going to reach him before he went inside so I continued blowing the horn until I was about 30 feet away, and still he didn't turn around. A car was just pulling out about ten feet from where Chet was standing and I whipped my car into it, parked, opened the door and called out to him, holding the flugelhorn high over my head for him to see.

"I've got the horn, Chet, look!" I said.

He stopped, turned around and saw me waving the horn over my head. He half turned, looked back toward the barbershop for a few seconds or so, then over to me. Short of tackling him and dragging him to the car, all I could do was hold up that horn. Another second or so and he walked closer to me. I lowered the horn and held it out a few feet in front of me.

"You told me you only owed the cat fifty, right?" I asked and Chet nodded. "Well he didn't let it go till after I had given him a hundred bucks!!" I said, pissed over having to do so. That got Chet's attention, which was good, since it stopped him from thinking about the barbershop.

"That motherfucker... I oughta go back and--"

"Listen to me, Chet. Forget about that asshole," I said, and held up the horn. "THIS is where it's at for you, man! Not in that friggin' rat-hole barbershop."

Chet looked back to the shop momentarily then started to rub his right arm with his left hand nervously. I'd come to know this indicated he was on edge. I didn't let up.

"Don't go into that fuckin' place, man. You know better than that," I said. I took out a pack of cigarettes, lighting one up for him and one for myself. He took in a long deep drag and exhaled slowly.

"Think about it, Chet. You're 40 years old, and you've got a beautiful wife and three wonderful kids. You can do one of two things. You can walk into that fuckin' barbershop and mess up the rest of your life and the lives of those who love and care for you. Or you can get into the car, take this horn and work your ass off, and find a way to get back into music where you so rightfully belong. It's all up to you, man!" I got back into the car and closed my eyes and said a silent prayer to almighty God that he would also get into the car and take the horn.

After a few moments, the passenger door opened and Chet

slid in beside me.

"I want to play again more than anything in the world, man," he said. I opened my eyes and handed the horn over to him. He lowered his head and rubbed the horn with child-like joy, so happy to have it again. In that pure moment of joy, he leaned across the seat and planted a kiss of thanksgiving on my cheek.

"I'll never forget this, man. I'll always be grateful to you for this, Art. I'm going practice until I get my chops back again--" He stopped abruptly, looked at me with a warm smile. "Thanks again, man."

"You don't have to thank me for anything. All I want is to see you back on top again! I'm going do everything I can to make that happen, too. And God willing, I'll do it."

"Thanks, Art," he said. To hear a guy like Chet Baker thanking me went straight into my heart. For me, it was truly an honor.

"Let's make it out of here," he said, a touch of anger in his tone. I think he was pissed that the cat had charged me an extra fifty bucks to get his flugelhorn back. I started the car and took off out of there and headed back to Redondo Beach. While we were driving along, Chet yawned and laid his head back against the seat and closed his eyes. I thought he was asleep so I automatically slowed the car down so I wouldn't wake him up. But then he opened his eyes, leaned forward in the seat and brought the horn up to his mouth and began to play some kind of scale in thirds. He was hampered by the movement of the car in traffic, so I told him to wait until I could find a place to pull over and park. I found a Thrifty Drug Store parking lot and pulled in around the far side where there weren't many cars, and parked.

"There! Now you can try it again, Chet," I told him, and he did. This time he played a couple of long notes. It was like he was seeing how long he could hold a steady tone, then stop when he ran out of breath, then do the same thing over again. He stopped, put the horn on his lap for a few moments, and then tried again. This time he played a ballad and managed to play nearly the whole tune, albeit a little hesitant, before having to stop due to numbness and pain. He looked at me for a few seconds then a warm smile broke out over his face, happy by what he had just accomplished. I was really happy for him and let him know it,

"I don't believe there's anybody in the whole fucking world that would even try to play with a loose-fitting bridge, you know what I mean, Chet? Like I said, you keep working till you get your chops back and when you're ready, I'll go to every club until I get you a gig. I promise you!" I meant it, too. That's how much Chet and his music meant to me.

He thought about what I'd said, and lowered the horn onto his lap and settled back in the seat looking to the road ahead in silence. Then, with a look of inner confidence in his eyes, without saying a word, he brought the flugelhorn up to his own eye level and just stared at it, as though he were studying it.

"Whatever it takes… I'm gonna play this horn again just like I used to, man," he said with conviction.

"I believe you, Chet. I really do." He put the horn down on the front seat, and brought his head back against the seat and closed his eyes, resting peacefully. I just sat there looking at him for a few minutes. Chet represented everything in jazz to me. I couldn't help feeling love, joy and sadness in my heart for this man. After another minute or so, I thought about taking Chet up to meet Nicky Blair, so I started the car and made my way into West Hollywood.

As I drove along Sunset Boulevard, Chet sat up and asked where I was going. When I told him, he said he really didn't feel right about meeting Nicky the way he felt just then. I asked him what he wanted to do. He held up his flugelhorn and said he felt like playing a little bit. We were only a couple miles from my house, so I suggested we go there.

I felt real happy for him. Now that he had his horn back, he'd found a new desire to overcome all the obstacles placed before him, and play again.

Chapter 13
Working Through the Pain

When we got to my house, Earla was glad to see Chet and learn that I'd bought his horn back for him. She asked him if he was going to play, and without another word, Chet sat down and began to play *Stella by Starlight*. After a few bars, though, he had to stop. He lowered the horn bell to his lap. He reached into his mouth, revealing the flimsy looking plastic bridge. He wiggled it back and forth.

"It's too loose, man," he said. Frustrated, he wiggled the bridge again. "The damn thing falls forward. Makes it hard for me to make a clean note."

It was plain he was tired, but said he knew he'd have to keep going over different tunes until he could get his chops in shape.

"And I have to try to find a stronger dental adhesive somewhere."

He managed a smile and brought the horn up to his mouth and tried again. He nearly played the whole tune, although a little uneven. But he was coming on, and it wasn't going to be long before he'd be playing whole melodies and beautiful solos again. And after that, five or six tunes back-to-back and doing full sets before a live audience.

He spent another hour or so with me, and in that time, Chet made attempt after attempt to play another complete tune until finally he was able to. But just about every time he played, he'd feel pain in his cheek and numbness along his jaw. Then he'd have to stop for a while, rub his jaw vigorously and then try again.

Chet had a lot of balls. That afternoon, after working for more than two hours, he played a little bit more. This time he was able to play rounder and cleaner notes, and his face was actually beaming.

About a week or so later, Chet had his mother's car and stopped by my house. He had his flugelhorn with him, and wanted to play a little, so he asked Earla and me if we'd mind.

"Don't be crazy, Chet, c'mon in," I said. He came in and sat down at the table. Earla asked about Carol and the kids and Chet smiled and told us they were all fine and thanked her for asking. He also told us how encouraging and supportive Carol had been. But he felt that maybe he'd been playing a little too much around the house lately, and didn't want to drive them up a wall, so he came to my house instead. I let him know that he was and would always be, welcome to come to our house anytime he wanted to practice or to play. I could see he felt comfortable and relaxed, so I asked him to come into the den, to play a little.

Once in there, he began by playing a tune called, *Solar*. I looked for my brushes but couldn't find them, so I took two matchbook covers. I was able to use them on the coffee table and make them sound like I was using brushes behind him. He glanced over and nodded, indicating that it sounded pretty good. When he finished the tune, we took a break. By this time, Earla had found my brushes under our bed and handed them to me. I got the L A. telephone book and accompanied him with brushes using the cover. He really liked that. He said we sounded good together - he was still playing a little rough, but his timing and his ideas were something else. After a few more bars, he stopped and let out a sigh. I believe it was because he was trying to play a little more each day and his chops were hurting.

He played another tune and he sounded pretty damn good, but again had to stop because of the obvious pain. After a few minutes, he started again. I watched in amazement as he continued to play, working his way through, adding note after note until finally he grimaced and had to stop. He gave a weary sigh and said he'd had it for the day. I was glad and told him that I didn't want to see him injure his mouth by playing for too long or too hard. He agreed, and said he had to be leaving soon anyway because it was getting late and he wanted to get his mother's car back to her at work, and get home to Carol and his kids.

He had a lot of chutzpah, and I knew that no matter what it was going to take, Chet was going to play again like he used to, even better. I personally witnessed the pain that playing for any length of time could bring on Chet. But I saw something else in the man. I saw absolute commitment, musical love and drive.

He played another tune, the one he'd tried to play the night when he and Carol had first come to our house, called, *I Love You*. And this time, the notes were cleaner, rounder and fatter.

We were happy and excited that he was playing clean, beautiful notes again, and would one day soon be able to play back-to-back tunes. He put the horn down and looked at me with a confident smile.

I told him how good I thought he was playing and he thanked me, mentioning again how much he really dug my brush play. He then asked if I could teach him to play a little. I was thrilled and excited that he asked and immediately got the telephone directory and brushes and started showing him how I played.

He was really impressed, wanting to know how I was able to use matchbook covers and brushes and play sensitive and delicate, yet strong, rhythmic and propulsive.

First, I showed him how I used my left hand by keeping it on the snare drum, in this case, the telephone book cover, in a continual rotating swirl, while my right hand played the same two, three, four pattern used on the ride cymbal. He especially liked the way I was able to use my left hand to accent and create a breathing roll, seemingly without breaking the continual swirling motion.

I handed him the pair of brushes, and not surprisingly, he picked up what I'd shown him almost immediately. I put on one of his records and he played right along. His time and rhythm were right on. He was a natural time keeper, and when I finally got a set of drums of my own, he would sometimes play them.

Chet spent a few more minutes with us and then said he had to go. Earla and I hugged him, and he left.

I had to leave, too and get to the grocery store and get food for our supper. On the way, I couldn't take my mind off how hard Chet was trying. I felt it would be nothing but a matter of hard work and time. And, true to his word, Chet was more than willing to give it all.

Chapter 14
The Wall

When I got back from the grocery store, Earla had a message for me from Nicky Blair. I called him back to find that he wanted to know if Chet and I would be able to knock down an old two foot wall which ran parallel to his driveway in order to create a clean pathway for construction to begin on the swimming pool he was having installed. He said we'd have to start on Monday morning because the construction crew would be arriving on Wednesday. I told him we probably could, but I'd check it out with Chet to make sure. The only thing I had to do now was to drive to Chet's house in the morning to find out if he was interested in doing the job with me, and if so, would he be physically up for the task.

I left early the following morning. When I got there, Carol opened the door. She told me Chet wasn't there. His friend, Norman, who worked in a local bakery, had come by earlier and picked him up and took him for a haircut. She told me I was more than welcome to come in and have a cup of tea with her and wait till he got back if I wanted to. I immediately took her up on her offer and went inside. Chet's mother, Vera, was sitting at the kitchen table with the three kids, showing them how to put together a new puzzle she had brought over for them. I said hello and watched them for a few moments. Vera looked up and smiled and asked if I wanted to join them. I laughed and told her no, because if I did, I'd probably be there all day long.

Carol had the tea all ready and invited me to join her on the couch. I always enjoyed talking with Carol. At times she'd tell me about her mother and father, and also her two other sisters, who I believe she said, lived somewhere in South Africa, and how one day she looked forward to visiting them.

As we were talking, I heard Vera tell the kids that she had

something to ask me before I left, and for them to keep working on the puzzle until she came back. She came over to me and seemed curiously interested in my background, quietly interrogating me, asking if I had ever smoked marijuana, taken LSD or heroin. I was a bit taken aback but assured her that I had never smoked marijuana or taken any other kind of drug because I always wanted to be in control of my mind and body. She smiled and said she was glad to know that. I got the feeling she wanted to know if I was someone who really cared about her son and wanted to help, rather than just some creep hanging around trying to take advantage of Chet's vulnerability.

I spent at least another hour and a half drinking tea and talking with Carol and Vera, but didn't want to bring up the topic about how Chet and I were planning to knock down a small wall the following week. Vera would no doubt be overly protective of her son by telling us that her Chetty shouldn't be doing that kind of work because he'd hurt his hands, or some other nonsense like that. Anyway, I got up and said goodbye to Vera and the kids. I shook Carol's hand, thanked her for her hospitality and asked her to have Chet call me when he got home.

Later that afternoon, Chet did call and I told him about the wall. It was an old, two-foot wall between 35 to 40 feet long, and held together by old cement. We could probably knock it down within hours. I also mentioned that we'd be making some pretty good bread for the job too. He was all for it.

A couple days later, I made a point of visiting Chet and Carol at their house. I wanted to make sure Chet still wanted to do the wall. Chet's mother, Vera, was there, so as soon as I got him away by myself, I told Chet I'd called Nicky and let him know that everything was going to be cool for Monday. He said that was cool and suddenly, began rubbing his nose. He clearly would soon be in need of a fix. Even though Vera probably knew Chet might still be taking drugs, he clearly didn't want his mother to see him this way and become worried. He asked me to take him to the store to get some groceries. I felt Chet wanted to show some respect to his mother, and, frankly, if it had to be done, I'd rather be the one taking him. At least, with me around the chances of him getting beaten up or robbed would be cut way down. And I sure didn't want to see anything happen to him with a family who loved and needed him.

We left the house quickly and I drove him to a house I hadn't been to before, and waited in the car until he came back. I was always relieved when he got back in the car, because, the state that shit left him in caused him to be so damn weak.

When Chet got in the car he leaned his head against the seat. He sort of dozed off peacefully knowing that he was safe with me. I waited until he came out of it and was fully awake, lit up a cigarette and passed it over to him. He thanked me and took in a deep drag and held the smoke in for a second or two and exhaled.

"You sure you feel up to knocking down Nicky's wall with me, Chet? I know you really need the bread, man, but it could turn out to be a pretty rough job."

He looked at me this weird, quizzical way but didn't say a word until we pulled up in front of his house.

"Don't worry man, everything will be cool. Besides, it'll be great exercise." He opened the door, stepped out and gave me this big smile. "See you Monday morning, man."

Most jazz musicians had, and still have, to do odd jobs in order to make a living. Most clubs only pay scale, plus most musicians don't play more than twice a week because there are so many of us. Unless you happened to be a big name, you just can't make a decent living as a jazz musician, and had to make up the difference with odd jobs.

Chet was at my house Monday morning around 8:30. We had a cup of coffee, and by the time we arrived at Nicky's house in the Canyon between Hollywood and Beverly Hills, it was going on ten o'clock. The moment Nicky saw us driving up to the front, he rushed out to greet us. I introduced the two and Nicky was absolutely thrilled to make Chet's acquaintance. He went on to tell Chet about how much he liked his music, and a bunch of other things, while I stood there listening and getting impatient because I wanted to get started on the wall.

Finally, Nicky started talking about the job, and as he's talking about it I could almost see the machinery of Nicky's brain working, looking at Chet, sizing him up, and wondering if Chet would really be up to the task.

"Are you sure you guys really want to do this? That's a pretty fucking long wall, Art. Maybe it's going to be too big a job for just the two of you to handle. Maybe I oughta get a couple other guys to help you out."

"No, don't worry about it, Nicky. We'll have the wall down in no time, right, Chet?" I said with cocksureness.

"Well, to do that we're gonna have to have a couple of sledgehammers to break through it, man," Chet said easily.

"You're right. Follow me," Nicky said. He led us into a big barn-like garage adjacent to the house where there was an array of tools. We each grabbed a 10-pound sledgehammer, a pick, and I grabbed the wheel barrel. We stuffed a couple of clean rags into our pockets and went back outside to figure out how we were going to attack the wall. Chet looked at the sledgehammer.

"Well, looks like we're going to be doing some hard time, Art."

Nicky and I got a laugh out of that. I lifted my sledge and noticed that the handle slid a little, and realized that if we weren't wearing gloves, we'd be left with some pretty damn sore blisters. I raised both hands to Nicky and asked him to get Chet and me a pair of lined gloves to protect our hands. He hit himself in the forehead, as if to say, 'what a dummy I am' and ran into the garage and came back with a pair for each of us. They fit perfectly. Chet removed his shirt and I noticed that he had a relatively muscular upper torso and developed biceps. I myself worked out faithfully three days of every week and was in fine physical shape. But I never expected to see Chet in such good shape.

"You been working out a little, man?" I said, impressed.

"Well, I guess you could call it that. I do a few push-ups now and then to keep myself in shape in case I might have to find some other line of work, you know?"

I turned to Nicky and told him he'd better leave so we could get started. He went into the house and Chet and I looked at each other, wondering which of us was going to start first.

"Go 'head Chet; you take the first whack at the wall." I said, extending my hand.

"Okay." He raised the 10-pound sledge over his head and with a lightning fast move, swung it forcefully into the wall sending a section of it flying out across the green lawn. He lifted the sledge again and hit the wall with vigor, causing another section to break off and fly onto the lawn. I lifted my sledge and struck the wall forcefully and likewise sent a section flying off. We kept this up for nearly fifteen minutes then stopped and took a breather. I had been right. The wall was old and in some areas it crumbled easily when struck with force.

Nicky came out carrying a jug of water and a couple of tall glasses and filled each one. We thanked him, drank the water right down and had another.

"If you need anything else," Nicky said, "just yell to me and I'll bring it out to you." He placed the water jug to one side and walked back toward the house, turning around briefly to watch us as we commenced striking the wall, sending chucks of brick, stucco and cement to the ground on the other side. With a satisfied look, Nicky smiled then went back into the house while Chet and I continued whacking away.

We knocked down a few more feet then stopped to take another break because the sun was getting hotter. I looked at Chet and asked again if he was okay. He nodded, reached into his back pocket and took out one of the rags to wipe his face and neck. Even though he was assuring me he was all right and was feeling strong and all, I was still going to keep an eye on him just in case. I'd never forgive myself if anything went wrong and Chet got injured.

Chet and I lit up a cigarette and sized up what we'd already knocked down. We both felt confident that we'd be able to finish the whole wall in a couple more hours or so. We finished our cigarettes and started slamming the wall again. The harder we slammed the wall the more the wall would split and crumble. We decided to continue on until we finished another few feet section before resting again.

About an hour later Nicky came back out again and offered us a cold beer but we both turned it down.

"I can't believe you guys have already knocked down so fucking much wall!" he said. He joked about how much of a mistake it would be for some loud mouth to mess with either one of us in a club, thinking we were nothing more than two weak-kneed jazz musicians. I agreed with what he said, but also let him know that we had a lot of wall left to do and it wouldn't get done if we just stood around shooting the shit. Nicky understood and quickly went back into his house.

Chet wiped his face and neck and I asked how he was holding up. He told me everything with him was cool, so I talked to him about a plan I had that would probably make it easier and faster for us to break larger sections of the wall down. We could stand a couple of feet away from each other and strike the wall in a sequential way. I'd go first and as soon as I struck the wall, he'd quickly follow, and in so doing we'd create a special rhythmic sort of thing, similar to what chain-gang prisoners used to do when pounding in railroad ties or splitting large rocks. I don't know why I hadn't thought of it before, but the important thing was I had, and wanted to put the plan into immediate action to see how it would play out. Chet shrugged casually said, "Well, let's give it a try, man."

I raised my sledgehammer, Chet raised his and then we started. The effect of the blows being so close caused large sections of wall to break off and crumble into pieces almost instantaneously. Without stopping, we exchanged excited looks and continued to whack that wall to smithereens until we had knocked down a good ten-foot section, and this made us both happy.

It was getting close to noon so we decided to take a break and headed for a shady area between Nicky's house and garage. Once there we sat down and lit up a cigarette. Just then, actor Michael Dante pulled up in the driveway and parked a few feet from us. He came over to say hello, saying he couldn't believe just the two of us were knocking down the wall. I didn't think he realized it was Chet Baker working with me, so I stood up and introduced them. They shook hands and it was easy to see there was an immediate feeling of mutual respect. They conversed for several minutes. Michael then excused himself, as he had a meeting with Nicky, but before leaving he mentioned how happy he was to have finally met Chet and looked forward to seeing him again.

After Michael went inside, I remembered the four bologna sandwiches I'd brought and went to the car to get them. Between the two of us, we dusted off all four sandwiches within two minutes. Nicky came out again and handed each of us a cold bottle of Fresca and man, we guzzled those babies down in seconds.

Nicky walked out to the wall and looked it over for a few seconds and came back amazed. He looked at Chet with concern.

"How are you doing, Chet? Are you okay?"

"I'm alright man, don't worry."

Nicky was satisfied and went back into the house. Chet and I lit up another cigarette and took a couple of drags, then he lowered his head and rested it on his knees. I looked at him resting there and still couldn't believe that the immortal jazz trumpet great, Chet Baker, and I were actually working with one another side by side. Of course, it wasn't what I'd imagined we'd be doing, but it sure was an unreal feeling.

I was used to doing this kind of work during the summer and fall months in Maine. I'd also worked on the re-facing of high dams using 50lb jack hammers, plus years painting houses. But poor Chet. I really wasn't sure how much hard work he had done before this, or how much longer he'd be able to go on. Before the day was over, I'd come to learn yet another thing about Chet Baker. This guy was really as tough as nails. He had an iron constitution and when he'd made up his mind to something, no matter how tough it was he would never throw in the towel. He'd be there 'til the end.

After a couple of minutes, Michael Dante came out, walked over and said goodbye to us. He told Chet it had been an honor to have met him, then left.

Chet then stubbed out his cigarette and walked to the wall, ready to go on the attack again. I watched him with utmost respect and then got up and walked over to join him.

We started again right where we left off, approximately a foot apart and facing each other. We had developed a rhythm and we were moving. As we were hammering away at the wall, two late model cars drove up and parked close to the house. I recognized the occupants in both cars. Nicky's beautiful movie star girlfriend, Angel Tompkins, drove the first car. James Aubrey, the former president of CBS Networks, drove the second. Chet and I took a quick breather when I mentioned who had just driven up to see Nicky, and how James Aubrey might just be the guy to help me get something going for Chet. Both Jim and Angel waved to me as they went into Nicky's house, and Chet and I resumed our battle with the rapidly disappearing wall.

As we continued sledging the wall in rhythm, I happened to look up and notice Chet's nose beginning to run a little. He quickly reached into his pocket and grabbed a small bottle, removed the cap and took a couple of swigs, then shoved it back into his pocket. He reached into his other pocket and brought out a small bottle of pills. He opened it and took out a couple pills and swallowed them with a drink of water.

"What was in that little bottle Chet?"

"Cough syrup with codeine… helps take away the pain."

"What about those pills?

"Pain pills is all. Got 'em from my doctor. They help cut the need for heroin."

"You sure you'll be alright to continue?" I asked with concern.

"I'll be cool in a few minutes. Let's just finish taking this fucking wall down, man."

So we continued on until we had completely broken up and demolished the wall without our ever having to use the pick.

"We did it, Chet. You're one hell of a strong cat! You're really something else, man!"

I looked at Chet, impressed that even though he'd been really hurting physically for most of the day from his body needing a fix, he stayed right with me every step of the way and never once wanted to quit before we finished what we had started.

Nicky came out to greet us as we made our way to the front of his house, looking beyond us to the now empty space where once stood a wall.

"I don't believe it!! You guys took this whole fucking wall down in a matter of hours!" he said in amazement. "C'mon inside and wash up. I'll put on a pot of coffee."

"We will, as soon as we get all this shit picked up first," I told him.

"Fuck it! Leave the shit there!" he said emphatically. "I'll have a couple guys from the restaurant take care of it in the morning. You guys go into the house and clean up. C'mon Chet,

I'll show you where everything is."

Nicky led Chet into the house while I picked up the sledgehammers and picks, placed them in the wheel barrel and took them back into the barn.

As I was coming back, I ran into Nicky. He wanted to know if Chet and I would be available to do some painting for him the next day at one of his bungalows in Westwood. I told him I'd check it out with Chet, and get back to him later that night at the restaurant. While we were alone I took the opportunity to ask Nicky if he could use some of his influence to get Chet on the Steve Allen show. At the time, I didn't know Chet had already been on the show some time earlier.

"You know everyone in this town, man. All the big name producers, directors and stars; they all come into your restaurant. Hell, you could pick up the phone and call Steve right now and get Chet a guest spot on his next open date," I said, hoping to butter up his ego. "You could do it just like that," I said, snapping my fingers. Nicky was listening, so I kept it up.

"He's playing better, and he really needs a break, Nicky. He needs to feel wanted, you know? Being seen on a show like Steve's would go a long way to prove to himself and others that he's still wanted and still has something to offer, you know what I mean? Right now he feels worthless."

Nicky stood there a few seconds weighing over what I said and started to nod his head. He looked at me and flashed a warm smile, and said he couldn't promise me anything, but he would give Steve a call and do everything he could to get Chet a spot on the show. I asked Nicky to promise he wouldn't let Chet know that I had asked him to call Steve Allen, because if he were to get on his television show I wanted Chet to feel that it was strictly Steve's idea and not mine or Nicky's. He gave me his word and the two of us went back inside his house, running into Chet who had just finished washing up.

I left the two of them there and went to get cleaned up. As I was going into the bathroom, I saw Nicky introduce Chet to Angel, and then to Jim Aubrey.

After I washed up, I went into the big living room. Jim and Chet were sitting across from one another holding a conversation and hitting it off very well. Jim was obviously very impressed with Chet. He was asking about some of Chet's songs that were his favorites, about some of the great musicians Chet had worked with, and so on. I was happy for Chet and decided to leave them to their conversation and went to find Nicky and Angel, a very beautiful blonde actress who had come to Hollywood from Chicago.

I had known Angel for a little over a year, having first met her in late 1967, a few months after I'd met Nicky. During my conversation with them, I segued into laying some future groundwork for Chet. I asked Nicky to throw some kind of not too strenuous work Chet's way so he could put food on his table for his family, maybe invite Chet up to the restaurant some night so Nicky could introduce Chet to some of the important movie stars, producers and directors who frequented his place. Nicky said he'd be happy to do that, and later, just as Chet and I were leaving, Nicky grabbed the moment and invited Chet, Carol, Earla and me to his restaurant the following week for dinner. And of course, we accepted the invitation gratefully. We exchanged handshakes with Jim and Angel and left for home.

On the way to my house Chet started telling me how much he had liked Jim Aubrey, but that he didn't know too much about the cat. I told him that Jim was one of the most powerful and influential men in the movie industry, and that one good word from him would carry an awful lot of weight, especially in the entertainment business. I really wanted to impress upon Chet the great need for him to practice, practice and practice, even if it meant having to play through numbness and pain. I told him to do whatever it took until he felt confident that he was good enough to play three full sets in front of an audience again. When he was, I would call everybody and anybody who was somebody, including Jim Aubrey, to come and witness his comeback performance.

Chet nodded and reassured me that he had every intention of getting himself back to the level of playing he once attained, no matter what it was going to entail. He didn't like to show much emotion, but when he did, you knew right away that he meant what he said and said what he meant.

The more I got to know Chet the easier it became for me to read his feelings. I learned, for example that every emotion Chet felt came pretty much through his eyes, because, with a single look he could invite or he could repel.

When we got to my house I invited him in for a few minutes but he had to get his mother's car back to her before 7:30pm. He lit up a cigarette as he got into his car, told me he'd see me in the morning and drove off.

The next morning came and there was no Chet. The phone started to ring and it was Nicky Blair asking where Chet and I were. I told him Chet hadn't arrived yet and I'd call him back when he had. I began to wonder why Chet hadn't shown up. He knew about the paint job we were supposed to begin that day. There was no way I could reach him by phone, so I decided to wait another half hour. If he hadn't shown up by then, I'd jump in my car and drive down to his house to see if everything was all right.

Just as I was about to get into my car, Chet shows up in his mother's car. When he stepped out of the car, I could see he had his horn with him.

"How come you gotcha horn with you, Chet? You gonna be playing it for Nicky while we paint?"

He smiled softly and told me he really didn't feel like painting today, but wanted to play some.

"Great," I said. "Let's go inside and I'll ask Earla to make us some breakfast." He said he wasn't hungry – all he wanted to do was play. I called and left Nicky a message that Chet and I wouldn't be at his house that day, and we went into the den.

Chet sat down and placed the mouthpiece into the horn and began to play different scales. The first thing I noticed was that he was able to play more notes and hold them out for longer periods of time. I was absolutely thrilled. He then played My *Funny Valentine* and the tone he was getting seemed different, a little darker and more poignant. I didn't know how he was doing it, but he was, and I was happy for him. He played for another ten minutes before stopping. I was curious about something Carol once mentioned, about how he'd play in the bathroom linen closet to keep the sound down. I wanted to know how that sounded and asked him about it. He said he'd show me.

He went into my bathroom and I followed. Chet shut the bathroom door and pulled opened the small linen closet door. He sat on the edge of the bathtub, placed the bell of the horn inside the closet and started playing a tune. The tone he got was amazing. The sound was different somehow, a little distant. It was like hearing music that was floating over the water from the other side, wispy and soft, yet clear, rich and full. What was unique about the sound was you could hear the air come through first, followed by the tone.

What was happening clearly showed the difference between a regular musician and a creative genius. Despite, and perhaps because of, the hardships and limitations in his life, Chet was forced to expand the boundaries of his talent as a jazz musician. Because he didn't want to disturb his neighbors, he started playing into the linen closet in the bathroom so he could control the volume, which led to a whole new tone. And because he was forced to find a new embouchure because of the ill-fitting bridge, he'd discovered an entirely new and lyrical sound.

After a while, Chet stopped playing and when he turned toward me, I noticed his upper lip was a little swollen. When he grimaced in pain, we went and sat down in the living room. Earla came out and made a pot of coffee and asked Chet if he wanted an ice pack for his mouth. He told her no, that the swelling just had to do with the rebuilding of his embouchure, and that he'd be cool in a few minutes.

I learned a lot about the determination and the artistry of Chet Baker that afternoon. He was keeping his promise, and I can honestly say that getting his flugelhorn back was the best thing I could have done for him.

Chapter 15
Nicky Blair Comes Through

A few days later, Chet came by the house and he was pretty damn excited to share some really good news with Earla and me.

The night before Chet had dropped by Stefanino's to say hello to Nicky. During their conversation, Nicky mentioned he'd run into Steve Allen at one of the big studios, and they'd started talking about jazz and jazz musicians. Nicky mentioned to Steve that he'd been introduced to Chet and Steve was very interested in know how Chet was doing. Nicky told Steve how he'd heard Chet was coming along well and playing better and stronger every day. When Steve heard that, his face lit up and asked Nicky to have Chet give him a call as soon as he could.

"So did you call him?" I asked excitedly.

Chet smiled happily. "Steve sent me a telegram and asked me to contact him," he answered. "So I called him," he said, and stopped talking. I was both curious and confused and asked him what Steve had said to him. Chet shrugged and said in a nonchalant tone that Steve just wanted to know if he'd be interested in doing a guest spot on his television show the following week. Again, he stopped talking, raised his eyelids and smiled playfully.

"So?" I asked impatiently. "What'd you tell him, Chet?"

He told me he was both happy and excited to say the least. At the same time, though, he was worried whether or not he was really ready to play in front of a national audience again. He put his hands together and placed his right thumb nail under his left thumb nail and moved them back and forth slowly, pensively. He did this sometimes when he was thinking something over carefully.

"So, are you gonna do it or what?"

He didn't say anything right away. But he didn't have to. I pretty much knew what he was thinking. Another few seconds passed.

"I'm not sure what I'm goin' to do yet, Art. Hell… I'm not even sure I can play a whole tune through, you know?"

"Of course you can, Chet," I said with confidence. "I've heard you do it when you're practicing." I had the feeling that even though he really needed the money, it was also terribly important for him to know and to feel good enough to play – to know if he still had a large enough fan base out there waiting to see him perform again.

We sat down and talked about it over coffee and a cigarette. I wanted to encourage Chet to use his performance on the Steve Allen show as a kind of measuring stick for him to see if he felt he would be ready to play in front of a live nightclub crowd. The vast difference between the two was that on Steve's show, he'd only be playing one tune, whereas in a nightclub format, he'd be playing six or seven tunes a set, sometimes eight or nine. So for three or four sets, we're talking about more than 20 to 25 tunes.

"I got an idea, Chet. Why don't you sing a tune and just play half a chorus?" I exclaimed.

He thought it over for a few seconds, smiled and said he thought it was a great idea and decided to go ahead and do the spot. I handed him the telephone and he called Steve and made the arrangements to do the show. While he talked to Steve, I went to my closet and brought out my new powder blue sports coat, and asked him to try it on. It fit him like a glove.

"Wear it when you do the show, Chet," I said.

He took the jacket off and folded it neatly over his arm.

"Thanks, man," he said softly, gave me a big hug and left the house.

I was thrilled. Can I say with absolute certainty that it was due to my suggestion to Nicky Blair that Chet got another spot on Steve's show? I don't know. But I do believe it helped set the wheels in motion.

A week later I was watching on television along with millions of others, as Chet performed on the Steve Allen Show. Chet sang a beautiful ballad called, *Forgetful*. It was just Chet with a rhythm section of piano, bass and drums. He called the time and began to sing.

"*Late....ly, you've been so forget...ful.... A kind of a stop....*" He then stopped abruptly and turned his head sharply around to his right in the direction of where the piano player was sitting, and shot him a nasty look, then turned back and continued to sing the rest of the lyrics with a look of consternation. After finishing the lyrics he brought the trumpet to his lips and played painfully, yet hauntingly to the bridge section. He then began singing the lyrics again bringing the tune to a close. He received a thunderous ovation when he made his way offstage.

It was then that the thought of why he had sung that particular tune hit me. It wasn't a famous standard like *My Funny Valentine*, or *Time After Time*. In fact, it was quite an obscure ballad written by Tadd Dameron, a personal friend and favorite composer of Chet's. The more I thought about it, the more it began to make sense. Let me say that I am not at all sure what was in Chet's mind when he chose to sing that particular tune. However, I had the gut feeling he'd chosen *Forgetful*, because he felt so many of his friends and fans had forgotten him. The song was his way of letting them know he was still very much around and kicking.

Chapter 16
Forgetful

The following afternoon I went out to Redondo Beach to visit. I was still excited about Chet's performance. When I walked in, the family was there, the kids watching cartoons, Carol and Chet sitting with them. Just a family at home, when the night before, Chet had been on national television. I wasn't so calm. I went over to the kids who pulled their attention away from the television.

"I want you to know that soon your daddy is going to prove to everybody who turned their backs on him how wrong they've been for giving up on him. Your daddy is going to make it all the way back to the top!"

They all smiled but really had no idea what I was talking about, and went right back to watching the cartoons. Chet smiled and shook his head. I asked Chet what it was that had pissed him off so much when he first started singing.

"I was up there trying to sing a beautiful ballad," he said, "and the piano player was layin' down a million notes behind me. I was upset, man. So I turned around, shot him a real icy stare, you know. The cat cooled it with all the notes after that."

I told him the most important thing that happened was the fact that he had sung and played on national television and had been seen by millions. That was an important start. I wanted to talk more about his performance when he asked me to take him to the store to buy groceries. He went over and kissed Carol, waved to the kids and we left the house.

Of course, what he really wanted was for me to take him to some guy's house somewhere in East L.A. so he could get himself what he called 'medicine' to alleviate his pain. I resigned myself to taking him. I kept telling myself that I could at least be there to make sure he didn't get into trouble, but I wasn't going to keep making it easy on him.

When we again ended up at Santa Monica Beach, I continued talking to him about how the drugs, in one form or another, were hurting him, and affecting the people that loved him.

"I'm not hurting anyone but myself, man," he replied. What was so frustrating to me was it seemed he genuinely believed he wasn't.

"But you are, Chet. You're hurting Carol, the kids, your mother, and me too. Think about it man, the bread you're spending to buy whatever shit it is you're buying, could be used for a lot of other things." I let the thought hang there. I knew I'd hit a nerve that time.

"Well…" he said softly, and remained silent for a while before speaking again. "Maybe you're right, man. I've got to start doing something." He took in a long breath. "I'll see my doctor about getting some stronger pain pills," he said, his voice drifting off.

"I really hope you do, Chet," I said firmly, wanting him to realize that time was moving on. We were fast approaching the New Year and he had to make some kind of move. "It's something you really got to start thinking about." I waited for a reaction. He looked me straight in the eyes, but didn't say a word.

"Listen, I set up a radio interview for you at KBCA-FM radio, the second Wednesday in December. Please promise me you'll make it for the interview. A lot of people will be listening to find out what you've been up to. And I'm going to call as many club owners as I can to hip them to this interview. A few of them might hire you for a comeback gig."

"Well, I wouldn't put much stock in that, man."

"Listen, 1969 is gonna be a whole different year, Chet. And who knows? Maybe this will be the year I get something happenin' for you. In any case, just make sure you're at my house before one o'clock on Wednesday. It'll take at least twenty minutes to get to East Wilshire Boulevard, and your interview is at two."

He promised to be at my house with plenty of time to spare and left it at that.

The day for Chet's KBCA-FM radio interview came and it

was a veritable downpour of rain. I glanced at the kitchen clock. It was nearing 12:45 p.m. and I was beginning to get real nervous. Earla came into the kitchen, looked outside and began shaking her head.

"Chet's not going to be able to drive all the way from Redondo Beach in this shitty weather just to do a two-bit interview. Forget about it, Art. Believe me, he's not going to show up."

"You don't know Chet very well. When he tells you he's going to do something or be some place, then you can bet your ass he'll do whatever it takes to keep his word."

"Maybe, but I wouldn't plan on it today."

I thought to myself that this time she could be right. There's a song that says it never rains in California, and when people think of L.A. the sun is always shining. But during the months of December, January and February the rains come down hard in L.A. I remember one year it rained steady for almost two weeks straight, and Earla didn't dare to drive to the grocery store. Californians can get like that. I also remember that the raindrops seemed to be as big around as a dime and when they hit you on the head, you'd really feel it. No ordinary person would want to drive in this kind of weather unless they absolutely had to. But then again, Chet wasn't your average person. He was a complete and total daredevil, fearing no one or nothing.

I looked out the living room window toward Washington Boulevard, some 200 feet from the house. What I saw next almost flipped me out and wanted my wife to see it, too.

"Earla, come in here quick! You've got to see this," I yelled. She came rushing into the room to see what I was so excited about.

Coming down the street was Chet and his two boys on a motorcycle, all three bareheaded and soaked. The cycle pulled into my yard and the three of them jumped off and ran into the house. As soon as they came inside, Earla directed the two boys into the bathroom, handing them each a towel, telling them to take off their wet clothes and dry themselves off, while she got them some dry clothes to put on.

Chet was clearly pissed and put out. He wasn't able to borrow his mother's car that day, but was able to borrow his friend, Norman's motorcycle. He said it was sunny when they left the house, so it wasn't a problem. But the rain had caught them completely by surprise just a quarter mile from my house. He'd only been going about 35 miles an hour, because he had the boys with him, and everything had been cool until the sudden rain. God bless him. He didn't have to explain anything to us. But I believe he wanted us to know that though he had a reputation for being a fast driver, when it came to his kids, he was a slow, careful driver.

I was about 5 feet 11 inches and Chet was perhaps an inch shorter than me, but could fit into most of my clothes easily. I gave him one of my shirts, a pair of dress slacks, and clean socks and told him to go into our bedroom to change. Within a few minutes he had dried his hair and changed into fresh clothes and came back into the living room. Earla said she'd take care of the boys and have all the clothes dry by the time we got back. Before leaving, Chet thanked Earla, and then we made our way to KBCA-FM Radio.

It was a wonderful interview, interesting and informative. Chet was questioned about how he'd been doing since the mugging and beating. Chet spoke about how hard he'd been working to re-learn how to play all over again, and re-develop the necessary facial muscles to make sound. The announcer asked how his daily life had been going, had Chet had any friends calling to check on him, or were any of them coming to his house to visit him? Chet answered him with unflinching honesty, telling him and the listening audience of Los Angeles that he had no telephone service, because it had been disconnected for lack of payment. He'd also had his electricity turned off for the same reason, and his mother paid to have it restored.

The announcer was sorry to learn of Chet's dilemma, and asked if Chet really believed he'd be able to overcome so great a tragedy and actually find a way to play again.

There was a space of at least 20 seconds of open air before Chet answered. He told him that a close friend had got him a flugelhorn several months ago and that he had been practicing hours every day. He was now able to play complete tunes, and felt he'd soon be able to sit down and play a few sets for his fans in the near future. The announcer was genuinely happy for Chet. The interview went on for nearly two hours with the announcer firing questions and Chet answering with great warmth and intelligence.

As I sat there in the adjoining room listening over the speakers, I began to cry. I cried because of Chet's painful honesty and the poignant manner in which he described his life. Here was a man who had just bared his very soul to an unseen listening audience, and not one of them had cared enough to call the radio station to say hello, or to wish him Godspeed.

As important as that might have been to both Chet and myself, the truly important and most significant thing to me about that afternoon was not the interview itself – it was about what the man had gone through in order to keep the appointment for the interview, as well as his personal promise of keeping his word to me. He had driven through a torrential rainstorm on a small motorcycle in order to make the interview. That's the kind of a man Chet Baker was!

There are those who didn't know Chet Baker up close and personal. They are the first ones to always say that Chet's word could not be kept or counted on, and other such bullshit. Well, for the record, Chet Baker always did whatever he could in order to keep his word.

As we made our way down the stairs to the outside parking lot, I couldn't help but notice the discouragement on Chet's face. He looked so defeated, and my heart went out to him. I knew the fact that no one had made a phone call to the station to ask him a personal question, or to tell him that they still loved his music had really bothered him. And yet, he didn't say a word about it. I opened the door to the parking lot and it was still raining hard. We ran over to the car and got inside as fast as we could. Chet still looked down so I made an attempt to get his mind focused on something else by asking him if he'd like to go get a coffee and a piece of apple pie. "Yeah, that sounds cool, man. I really haven't had a thing to eat all day."

"Where do you want to go, Norm's on La Brea, Musso and Frank's on Hollywood or Denny's on Sunset?"

"Well, we might as well make it to Norm's."

"Norm's it is then." I found an alleyway, made a turn and drove west on Sunset to the restaurant. Inside we found a booth at the far end and ordered coffee and cheeseburgers, followed by a piece of fresh-out-of-the-oven apple pie. Chet seemed and looked okay, but at that point in time, I was never quite sure. I asked him if he felt all right, or if he needed any medicine, as I always referred to it in public. But he said no, he was feeling pretty good. I really felt conflicted over Chet's drug use. On the one hand, I really wanted to see him kick the habit, while on the other, it hurt to see him in pain. I didn't want to have him vulnerable to hoodlums or suffer through going cold turkey. I had no experience with knowing what was the best thing to do. All I knew was that right now he was feeling low. I didn't want to hurt his feelings by talking about the interview, but I had to let him know how pissed off I felt that nobody had called. Chet just brushed it aside.

"Well… when you're in demand, you've always got people hanging around. When you're down…" he stopped, rolled his eyes and shrugged his shoulders. "The world turns its back on you, man, and nobody wants a thing to do with you, you know?" He smiled like he was trying to convince me that it hadn't bothered him, but it was painfully evident that he couldn't cover his inner hurt.

"To hell with them all, Chet, because pretty soon, you will be playing in a decent club, and when you are, people WILL come out and support you, I just know it. You'll start recording again, and every one of those bastards out there who gave you up for dead will come out of the walls like cockroaches and tell you how great you are, and how happy they are to see you back, and all that other kind of bullshit. You just wait, man."

"Getting a record deal would be great, Art. But I don't believe you're going to find any record producer willing to take a chance on me, or any club owner for that matter. They think I'm just too much of a risk for them. And maybe I am," he said with a dejected shrug.

"Well, it really doesn't matter what they think anyway, Chet. As soon as you feel you're ready to play in public again, I'll start making the rounds and let everybody know you're making a comeback. That should draw a lot of attention, don't you think, Chet?"

"Well, I don't know, Art. I hope so," he said with an air of skepticism. He told me about the people who claimed to be friends and had promised to help him, but that when he called on them, all they had for him were excuses. Hearing him say that helped me understand his reason for not becoming overly excited about my plans to get his career jump started again.

We sat there for a few more minutes looking out of the window to the falling rain, and I could see that Chet was getting tired. We paid the check and made our way through the driving rain and into my car. I hadn't driven more than 100 feet before Chet was sound asleep. I didn't want to hit any bumps that would cause him to wake up suddenly, so I just drove 35 to 40 miles an hour until I got to my house in Culver City. As soon as I pulled into my yard, Chet woke right up refreshed, and we both ran through the rain into the house.

Earla had Chet's boys all dried off and dressed in their own clothes. They were on the floor playing with our three kids. Chet and I had a cup of coffee, then he gathered his boys together for the long ride home. Outside, the rain wasn't letting up so I suggested he leave the motorcycle in my garage and I'd drive them home. He could pick up the bike the following day. He immediately like the idea and decided to take me up on my offer. I drove Chet and his sons back to Redondo Beach. When I pulled up, the rain had just about stopped. Chet asked me if I wanted to come in for a while, but I need to get back home.

Then in a very serious tone, Chet turned to me. "I really value our friendship, man. It really means a lot to me, you know?" I reached across the seat and gave him a friendly slap on the shoulder.

"Thanks, Chet. I feel the same way." I slapped him again, adding, "I'll always be here for you, man. I want you to know that, you dig?"

He smiled, got out of the car and followed his boys into the house.

One thing about living in L.A. back then was that all the driving on the freeways gave you plenty of time for thinking. On my way home that afternoon I thought about what I was learning about Chet. It felt like an absolute gift from God that I was becoming a friend to the man whose music touched my heart so deeply. I came to learn much later on that Chet revealed things to me he would never have told others.

He confided to me in no uncertain terms, how he'd felt a kinship to me, and could trust me. Knowing that gave me great comfort because, unlike myself who had six siblings, Chet had no brothers or sisters that he could really feel free to talk with about his own personal troubles or trials. Like a brother, I became that confidant.

It was clear that Chet had studied me, my actions and responses to him. This was a necessity for him as it was how he would test people to see if they could be trusted. And I had observed many of Chet's nuances. For example, I learned what to look for that would let me know when he was getting tired, bored, anxious or upset. He'd do certain things with his hand, like running a hand over his cheek, or along the bottom of his jaw. His face was a road map of emotion that unconsciously displayed all the pain, pathos and poignancy felt deeply within, which found escape and expression through the bell of his beloved trumpet.

Chapter 17
Methadone and Compassion

A few days later, I was up pretty early and decided to drive down to Redondo Beach to see how Chet was doing and to spend more time with him. Just before getting there though, I stopped at the little variety store and picked up a half gallon of milk and a loaf of fresh bread and a pack of Pall Mall cigarettes, just in case they might have a need of one or all three.

When I got to the house Chet's mother, Vera opened the door and let me in. She always seemed happy to see me, always had a smile for me.

"Art's here, Carol."

Carol was seated on the couch with little Missy, who was drawing. Missy looked up at me with those big brown eyes and explained that her Daddy was in the back yard playing with Paul's toy. Carol smiled and pointed to the glass sliding door, which led to the patio. I nodded and made my way to the sliding glass door that opened to the small patio area. I slid the door open, stepped outside, and there was Chet, sitting on the cement, totally engrossed and focused on repairing some small toy. He wasn't even aware of my presence until I asked what he was doing. His whole body flinched. He jerked his head and looked up at me in surprise.

"Man! You scared the shit out of me! I didn't even hear you," he said softly and took in a deep breath. "Oh, it's just a Tonka Toy truck Paul got last Christmas. One of the kids left it out in the yard next to the street and some car came by and ran it over." He held the little red truck up and I could see where the front section of the toy had been dented in, and how Chet had somehow managed to make the dent nearly disappear.

He gathered his small array of tools and stood up, and the two of us went inside. He walked over to Vera, who had joined Carol on the couch, and showed her what he had done with the toy. She told Chet how happy Paul would be when he saw that his father had repaired the little toy truck. Vera turned, smiled and looked up to Chet,

"Just like the time you were so happy when your father spent half a day fixing your little red toy car too. Do you remember that, Chetty?" she asked, somewhat teary-eyed. Chet looked at me for a few seconds, then to his mother, and smiled, remembering.

"Yeah… I do remember that little red car and dad fixing it," he answered. He looked at the small red toy truck in his own hand for a few seconds. "Guess you were right, ma," he said. She looked at him, wondering what he was talking about. "It took me almost three hours to pry the dent out of this little toy truck," he said, the words dying on his tongue.

Carol was curious about why Chet had stopped talking and asked what could be troubling him.

"Well…" He hesitated again and Carol looked confused. But Vera knew.

"I believe what Chet is trying to say, is that he realizes that it takes love and patience to want to make things right, even something like fixing a little toy." She looked to Chet again, sighed, and raised her glasses to wipe away a tear. "Isn't that it, Chetty?"

He didn't answer, but she went on. "Your father really did love you. Otherwise, he never would have taken the time to fix something he knew would make you happy, like you did for Paul here. Your father did love you, Chetty. He just didn't know how to say it."

Chet tried to make light of the comparison, but I could see it in his eyes. He knew in his heart that his father loved him. The atmosphere was getting too sentimental for Chet and he reacted. He looked at Carol.

"Art's taking me to see a friend of his near MacArthur Park, and from there, we'll be going back to Art's house for awhile." He leaned over and kissed Carol then Missy. "I should be back between 4:30 and 5 o'clock. See you later, ma," he said.

Well, of course, we weren't really going to see a friend of mine. Chet asked me to drive him to an address near MacArthur

Park. Once there, I parked and glanced at my watch. It was close to noon. Chet looked around for a few seconds then got out.

"What house are you going to, Chet?" I was concerned, because this was considered a tough neighborhood also. He pointed to a three-story, gray house trimmed with white.

"Cat lives on the first floor rear, on the right coming in." He smiled. "Nothing to sweat with this cat though. It'll be cool. Be back in a while." He left me and walked hurriedly across the street. I watched him until he disappeared into the apartment building, then I lit up a cigarette and sat there watching the people walk by, each focused on their own private world.

Across the way, I could see a lot of people walking around the huge pond of water in the middle of the park, and a lot of them seated on the grass at water's edge, feeding the pigeons on land and the birds in the water. I looked back at the apartment house where Chet had gone and everything looked cool. As I turned back around to look over to the park, there were two men, shabbily dressed, dirty and unshaven, staring into the car at me.

"You got any loose change you can spare, mister?" one of the men asked. As I was reaching into my pocket to check, the second one leaned his head inside the car. "All we need is enough to git somethin' to eat. We ain't eat'n a thing in three days." He then pulled his head back outside into the open air, looked up the street, pointed to a two-story building about a hundred feet away and said that was where he and his friend sold their blood for money.

The building looked very familiar to me. The man told me that his friend was paid fifteen bucks for his blood a few days ago, and that he had only been given eight bucks for his own. I felt an immediate pull on my heart for these two men because I knew exactly what it was like to have sold one's blood for money.

The first time Earla and I moved to L.A. back in 1963, the only money I had was just enough to rent a small house, and after that, nothing to buy food with. I picked up a Los Angeles Times newspaper and read the 'Help-Wanted' section and came across an advertisement about some blood bank in downtown L.A. paying upwards to $25 for a pint of blood. So I went, sold a pint of my blood and was paid something like $14 bucks. The first thing I did with the money was buy food for my family. All I could get for work at that time was 'day jobs' and that didn't pay a hell of a lot. And as far as working in the club scene in L.A., it was a tough place to get work as a jazz musician at that time. So I was forced to go back to the blood bank and sell another pint. And sure enough, this was the exact same building. The Bible teaches, "It is more blessed to give than to receive." I reached into my pocket gave each one of them a dollar. I felt the presence of God in my heart. It was a sensation of absolute peace combined with the scent of violets and cedar.

A few minutes later, Chet appeared, saw the men standing by the car, and gave them a quick once over.

"Everything all right, Art?" he asked with concern.

"Yeah, everything's cool! They're just looking for a little help so they can get a bowl of soup and a few crackers."

Chet didn't really have any kind of money, but he reached into his pocket and handed each one of the men all the change he had on him. The two homeless men were very grateful, thanked us, and then made their way down the street, stopping to ask other passers-by for a handout. Chet and I watched the reactions of all who were stopped and asked for a handout. The people reacted as though they had been insulted, like they were far above the two homeless men, and wanted nothing to do with them. I watched with pity as the two men made their way over to the park and disappeared behind the tall palm trees.

"That's one of the things I could never understand about people."

"What's that, Chet?"

"How they can just turn their backs on somebody in need," he answered with disdain. I looked at him and thought about what he'd said, and of course, he was absolutely right.

This wasn't the first time I'd seen Chet reach out to someone in need. On one of our visits to Santa Monica Beach, some poor bum came up to us and asked if we had some loose change he could have. Both of us reached into our pockets and handed the guy something like a buck-and-a-half in change, and he couldn't thank us enough. I figured he'd leave after we'd given him some change, but he didn't. Instead, he just stood there talking and telling us how nice we were and all, then dummied up as he looked out toward the street. Chet and I looked up at almost the same time and saw a police cruiser pull up to the curb and park directly in front of where we were seated and talking with the man. The cop got out, looked our way and started walking toward us. The poor homeless man looked at me then to Chet, a look of panic in his eyes. He begged us to help him, and told us his name was Bill and that he lived in some abandoned house in Venice Beach, and that if the cop thought he had been begging for money, he'd be put in jail and didn't have any idea when he'd be let out. He asked if we would please tell the cop that we knew him so wouldn't be arrested. Chet and I exchanged looks and both our eyes said the same thing, there was no way we could refuse to help this poor guy.

The cop walked up to the man, and without warning grabbed him roughly by the arm and started to handcuff him. When he did that, both Chet and I jumped up immediately.

"What the hell are you doing, man? This guy's our friend. He's not doing anything wrong, man!" Chet said with firmness.

"That's right, officer. He's with us," I echoed.

The cop speared us a look like he knew we were bullshitting him, and asked who we thought we were kidding, telling us that the man was nothing but a bum. He told us he'd seen the man taking money from us as he was driving by, and that had been his reason for stopping in the first place.

As though the two of us were on the exact same wavelength, Chet told the cop that he was wrong, our friend was not a bum and we were not giving him money, it was the other way around. He went on to tell the cop that the man was giving us back the change he owed us from the cigarette money. The cop looked at Chet dubiously, then at the homeless man and then over to me. The look on his face told us he wasn't buying what we were telling him and asked if we really expected him to believe that we really knew the man. He asked us what the bum's name was and we simultaneously answered that his name was Bill. The cop looked surprised then asked for the bum's last name and Chet told him that he didn't really know the man's last name but simply knew him as Bill.

"He's right," I affirmed. "I asked Bill if he'd mind going to the store to get me a pack of cigarettes." As I was telling this to the cop, I reached into my shirt pocket and took out an unopened pack of Lucky Strikes, which I had bought a half hour before, and held them up to show the cop. "As you can see officer, it's a brand new pack. And Bill here was just giving us back our change, not bumming from us."

The cop looked at Chet, to me, and the homeless man, a look of confusion written across his face. He then turned and walked back to his car scratching the back of his neck as he did so. He got into his cruiser, looked back to us and drove away.

Bill, happy and relieved, shook each one of our hands, and thanked us again. We told him that it wouldn't be wise for him to hang around the area because that cop might get wise and come back. He agreed and thanked us yet again, and walked off in the general direction of Venice Beach, turning around several times to wave to us.

Chet didn't have much, but he would willingly give what he had to a stranger in need.

As we sat in the car at MacArthur Park, smoking cigarettes, I noticed Chet wasn't behaving the way he usually did after he'd copped something.

"Wasn't the guy in?" I asked curiously.

"What guy?" he answered, a bit confused.

"The one you went to see in that building over there. Wasn't he there?"

"Yeah, he was there, why?"

"Because you're not acting like you usually do after seeing one of those cats."

He quickly figured what I was talking about and explained that he and Carol had been having some real serious thoughts about his use of drugs and that he was going to try his best to stay away from the hard shit, and stay on pain pills. I really believed him because there was a strong determination in his tone of voice. He went on to say that all he'd had that day was a few painkillers, and that the man he had just seen across the street had sold him a new drug called Methadone, a synthetic substitute for heroin.

"It's been around in England for quite a while. I was on it one time." Apparently, this new treatment was starting to become available here in the U.S.

"How do you use it? What's it supposed to do for you?"

Chet explained that the methadone was designed to stop the craving for heroin. "If there's anything that'll help me to kick the shit, I'm willing to try it," he said. The guy Chet had been to see had given him the address and phone number of a doctor who was willing to help out.

Clearly, he was telling me the truth because he was fully awake and aware. I was also happy to know that he was going to a doctor about getting this new medicine. It really upset me to see the effects heroin had on him.

We left and went to my house so Chet could make a couple of phone calls. While Earla made coffee, Angel Tompkins dropped by to see about a dress Earla was designing for her. Chet and I said our hellos, then left the two of them and went into my den. Chet had brought his horn along and wanted to play. I played brushes along with him and we played jazz standards at various tempos. He sounded just great, but after a while he had to stop because of the pain in his jaw. I was glad to see his focus and determination to stay on track and was hopeful this new synthetic drug would help.

Chapter 18
Arrest and Deliverance

Though my friendship with Chet was becoming an important part of my life, much of my time was spent painting houses in the daytime and a lot of my nights at Stefanino's where Nicky would introduce me to people in the entertainment business. Equally important was spending a great deal of time with my three children. Every day after school, I'd play pass football in our backyard with my eleven-year-old son, Arthur, and Monopoly with him and my eight-year-old daughter, Rhonda. And though she wasn't quite old enough to actually play the game, we always included my three-year-old daughter, Kathy. And on nights when I wasn't out playing drums, I'd spend hours watching television shows with them. On special nights I'd take them up to Stefanino's. Nicky would treat them like royalty. He was beautiful that way. Earla and I used to take the kids to Disneyland at least once every week, usually on weekends when I'd finish a paint job and would have extra money to spend. We tried most of the rides but our very favorite was 'It's A Small World" - a boat ride through a long water tunnel with kids from around the world singing the song in their own language. I probably enjoyed these things as much as my kids.

The Saturday after taking Chet to MacArthur Park, I was playing 'Hot Wheels,' a toy car game with my kids. They were having the time of their lives. The phone started to ring, so Earla answered it. Chet wanted to speak with me. I left the kids racing the cars and went to the phone.

"Yeah, what's happening?" When he answered, his voice was softer than usual, and he sounded nervous. He said that he really needed my help, and could I come over to pick him up. Well, my first thought was that maybe something had happened to

Carol or one of his kids, so I asked him if they were all right. He assured me they were fine, but that had not been his reason for calling me. He'd been arrested. He was in the Gardena jail, and was allowed to make only one call, so he called me and wanted me to get over there as fast as I could, otherwise the Gardena police would keep him locked up until Monday. And he was emphatic in saying he didn't think he could take it that long without help.

"JAIL??!!! What jail? What the hell are you doing in there? What happened?"

He told me that after he'd talked with me at the park, he was in pain and had driven over to Hawthorne to make contact with some kind of doctor. He told me how he had found the doctor's house somewhere between Hawthorne and Gardena, and how the doctor had given him an injection of some kind of synthetic drug which had left him feeling weak and very woozy, and that it had almost the same effect as real heroin.

"Don't tell me you tried to drive back to Redondo Beach after the shot, Chet." There was a brief silence. "You didn't drive, did you, Chet?" I knew that he must have, otherwise he wouldn't be in jail, but I had to ask him anyway.

He said that he had and that while driving he had fallen asleep and had sideswiped two parked cars but hadn't stopped to check it out. He said the next thing he knew he had been pulled over by the Gardena Police and then arrested and charged with DUI and leaving the scene of an accident. I told him to be cool and I'd be there to pick him up as soon as I could. I heard some cop's voice in the background order Chet to hang up, and within seconds, the loud sound of the phone being slammed into its cradle rang in my ears.

About fifteen minutes later, I received another call and it was from Carol. She had spoken with the police. They informed her that the tests conducted on Chet the night before had determined he was under the influence of a synthetic drug prescribed by his doctor. The DUI charged had been dropped; Chet wouldn't have to go to court and would be released later that day. I assured her that I'd pick him up.

I arrived at the Gardena police station just before 6:00pm, and spoke with the officer on duty, telling him I was there to pick up my friend, Chet Baker. The cop looked at a stack of papers on the counter top, fumbled quickly through them and pulled out a particular sheet, looked it over for a few seconds, then casually placed it back and told me to wait. He went behind a small wooden partition and within a few seconds, he was back and Chet was with him. He came out from behind the partition and gratefully put his arms around me. I asked the officer for the details of Chet's arrest. He said a woman called the station early Friday evening and reported that she had witnessed a car strike two different parked cars and drive on without stopping. She'd written down the license number, and Chet was picked up and arrested for DUI and with leaving the scene of an accident. I asked if there had been any injuries and was told that both cars had been unoccupied at the time, and because of that the charge of leaving the scene had been dropped as well, and Chet was free to leave. We waited while the officer gathered Chet's personal belongings, and once Chet had them, we left the station, got into my car and drove off.

Chet looked tired and weary and then all of a sudden, his nose began to run and he became nervous and anxious. He asked if I had any kind of painkillers in the car.

"No man," I answered. "All I've got is cough syrup, in the glove compartment, there." He opened the compartment, found the small bottle of cough syrup, read the label hurriedly, then brought the bottle to his mouth and quickly swallowed the entire contents down in two swallows, then breathed a long sigh of relief.

"Thank God you had the cough syrup. I was probably just minutes away from having to go cold turkey again. The codeine will calm my nerves until I get home." I sure as hell didn't want to have to see him go through cold turkey. I had seen Chet in a bad way a couple of times, and suffice it to say, it sure as hell wasn't a pretty sight to see. We hadn't driven more than five miles when Chet realized he didn't have his wallet. In his haste to leave the jail, he had forgotten to ask the officer for it. So, I turned the car around and drove back. Something made me nervous about the whole thing, like something was going to happen if Chet went back into the police station.

"Maybe you'd better wait in the car and I'll go in and get it, what do you think?"

"No... I'll have to go in and get it myself because they won't know who you are."

We went inside and walked up to the counter. The cop, who had released Chet some twenty minutes ago, was no longer on duty, and in his place was another officer, this one was a sergeant. He gave the two of us the once over and asked what our business there was. Chet told the sergeant that he had been released some 20 minutes earlier and had forgotten to take his wallet.

"What's your name?" the cop asked gruffly.

"Chesney Henry Baker."

The sergeant turned around, walked a few feet to some desk, opened the top drawer and brought out a dark brown wallet and looked through it. He was about to pass it across the counter but noticed some papers on his desk and stopped to look them over. Then he looked back at us with a curious look. "Are you Chet Baker, the musician?" he asked.

"Yes sir," Chet answered proudly. Without another word the sergeant came out from behind his desk and grabbed Chet roughly by the arm, turned him around and placed handcuffs tightly over his wrists.

"You're under arrest!" he said. Chet was totally bewildered and confused.

"For what?" he asked incredulously. "I just got out of here."

"Well you're back under arrest now. There's an outstanding warrant here, that's all I know," the sergeant told him. Chet looked at me with a look of helplessness.

"Do something, Art. See if you can reach Herb!" he yelled out. It really didn't hit me until later what he'd meant by that, because I was in shock myself. All I wanted to know was what the warrant was all about.

The sergeant said something to the affect that Chet had failed to appear in court for unpaid parking tickets. I couldn't believe it. Chet arrested for not paying parking tickets. He must have had a hell of a lot of tickets for a warrant to be issued. But knowing Chet, he probably paid no attention to the tickets or the accumulation of how many he'd actually received. But that was academic, because here he was, being re-arrested within a period of a half hour, and I couldn't do a thing to help him.

The sergeant took Chet by the arm and led him to the cell area. I waited until he returned to his desk so I could ask him what I could do to get Chet released. I knew if he had to spend another 24 hours in jail he'd be going through a cold turkey stage. I was told I'd have to post his bail, or collateral equaling the amount. I didn't have either and knew I'd have to find somebody that did and immediately.

I left the police station and drove home, racking my brain on the way trying to figure out who the hell I could get to put up the bail money. And then I realized what Chet had meant about me trying to reach Herb. He was talking about Herb Alpert. I didn't know Herb personally, but figured if Chet wanted me to call him, then I was sure as hell going to call him; Herb would no doubt put up the bread for bail. Hell, with all the juice Herb had, all he'd have to do was pick up a phone, call any bail bondsman and tell him that he wanted Chet out and Chet would be released immediately. I got to my house just after seven o'clock in the evening and called A&M Records, but Herb had already left for the day. I tried calling Nicky Blair at his house and restaurant but was told by Pia that he'd gone to Vegas to see Frank Sinatra and wouldn't be back until Monday.

I decided to try Hal Cohn, a man I'd met recently at Nicky's restaurant. Hal was a music promoter and managed a well-known rock group. He was a big friendly guy and a major fan of Chet's who had also expressed a strong desire to meet him in person. So I called Hal, explained the situation, and before I had even mentioned the word bail, he gave me his address and asked me to come pick him up at his place in Hollywood. I told my wife and she gave me her blessings and I left the house.

I picked up Hal and drove to Redondo Beach to pick up Carol. I explained to her who Hal was and filled her in on what was taking place and why she'd have to come with us to the Bail Bondsmen's office to verify that she was in fact, Chet's legal wife. Carol went next door to the neighbor's and called Chet's mother, who quickly came over to take care of the kids while the three of us went to bail Chet out.

We drove to downtown L.A. to see a friend of Hal's who was a bail bondsman. That completed, I dropped Carol off at her home because Vera had to get up early the following morning and go to her job.

Hal wanted to go with me to the Gardena police station because he was all excited about meeting Chet in person. I figured, why not, it was the least I could do. After all, he did step up and pay for Chet's bail. On the way over to the station I talked to Hal about my trying to get Chet a gig in just about every place in L.A., from the Playboy Club to a strip joint on Sunset. He said he had a few connections and would see what he could come up with.

I pulled up and parked in front of the police station and asked Hal to wait in the car while I went inside to get Chet. Once inside, I walked up to the desk sergeant on duty and told him why I was there. He told me to cool my heels while he checked it out. A few minutes went by and then the sergeant returned and Chet was with him. As soon as Chet saw me his eyelids flickered and his eyes lit up like halogen lights on a pitch-black night. He said goodbye to the officer and we took off out of there like deer running from a forest fire.

Chapter 19
On the Comeback Trail

When we got inside the car, Chet noticed Hal seated in the back seat and looked at me warily wondering who the guy was. I introduced him to Hal and told him that it been Hal who had put up the bread for his bail. Chet relaxed a bit, and thanked him, then asked me if I had a cigarette. I gave Chet one, Hal had his own and we all lit up and I drove off

Hal soon began a conversation with Chet about a gig that he and I had talked about setting up for Chet.

"Art has been filling me in on all the shit that's been happening to you the past couple years," he began. "First of all though, I want you to know that it's a real honor for me to actually meet you in person, Chet." Without turning around, Chet thanked him warmly.

I told Hal about how many clubs in L.A. and Hollywood I'd gone to and talked to the managers about getting a gig for Chet and how each one of those bastards turned me down cold. I told him how I had even tried to get a gig for him at the Melody Room, the rock joint on Sunset and Larrabee. Hal said he knew the owner real well and could get him a gig there. So I asked Chet if he'd be interested.

"Well… might be all right. What do you think the bread would be like, Hal?"

Hal told Chet the money wouldn't be anything close to what he'd been accustomed to getting, but at least it would let all the record producers, club owners and musicians in the area know that he was back playing again. Hal told us he would talk with the owner about having Chet there sometime after the holidays. Hal went on to say that once he had cemented the gig, he'd get back to us.

"Yeah, Chet, we could announce it in the papers as 'Chet

Baker's Comeback Performance,' and I'll bet the place will be packed." Chet thought it was a great idea and said he'd think it over.

Hal lived in Hollywood, so I decided it would make sense for me to drive the three of us to Denny's on Sunset for coffee and conversation then drop Hal off at his place afterwards. Ten minutes later we were seated in Denny's, and Hal brought up the subject about how he would like to be Chet's manager. Chet immediately squashed the idea and firmly told him that he didn't trust anybody but me. This was especially true after what he and Carol had been put through with his last agent, a man from New York City whom Chet referred to as the cheapest son-of-a-bitch he'd ever come in contact with. So any ideas that Hal had about getting the chance to manage Chet were completely shot down.

Chet wasn't trying in any way to hurt Hal's feelings, especially after his gestures of kindness, so he went on to explain how the agent had taken full advantage of his trust by signing Chet's name on a recording contract to cut five albums and Chet was never paid a single penny for his work, or royalties of any kind. The agent kept the money and failed to pay for his hotel bill so that when he and Carol had returned from a tour, they found that they no longer had a room to come to and found that all of their clothes and other things had been carelessly put out on the sidewalk in front of the hotel.

"Nothing personal man, I don't trust anyone, except for Art here, you know?" Hal nodded his head indicating he understood. "It really doesn't matter where I make my comeback, man. The people will either come to see me, or they won't, you know?" he said matter-of-factly.

The three of us shook hands on it and began to set our plans in motion. Hal was a very confidant man and had a lot of contacts. He told Chet that as soon as he got the Melody Room gig cemented, and we took it for granted he would, Hal would buy a full page spread in the L.A. Times, The Examiner and one in Variety, to help promote his comeback. Hal also mentioned that he might even throw a champagne buffet party and invite the press, a few hip stars and famous musicians in the hopes of getting people to come out in support of Chet.

Chet seemed pleased by this. "Well... we'll do the gig and see what happens, Art."

"You mean you want me to play?"

"Yeah, you're going to be doing the gig with me, man," he said matter-of-factly.

"Okay, but you've never heard me play!"

"Yes I have, man. The way you play brushes is out-of-sight. I've been digging the way you've been playing along with me on that telephone book in your den, man. You've got big ears and great time," he said, and smiled. "That says enough to me."

I was really happy that he had chosen me to be the drummer on his comeback performance. I mean I had managed to sit in and play two or three times a week with a lot of the names musicians in the L.A. area just to keep my chops up and my name alive. Chet could have hired a better-known drummer, yet he chose me.

"I haven't been playing that much lately, Chet. But you KNOW I'll be up for that, man," I said with quiet confidence.

"I know you will, Art," he replied. I didn't want to let on to him how excited I was about finally getting the chance to play with him. Now all I had to do was pray that Hal Cohn would get Chet the gig, and my long awaited hope would become reality.

As the three of us sat there talking, another reality suddenly hit me, the fact that I didn't own a set of drums. I decided not to say a word about it then, but would talk to Chet about it when I drove him home. We finished our coffees and left. I took Hal home first because he lived in the area. Driving Chet home, I asked what was I going to do about getting a set of drums. He told me not to worry, that he'd get a set for me. I figured he knew where he could borrow a set for me, so I put the thought out of my mind.

December had passed into the new year when, in January 1969, I got a call from Hal telling me to inform Chet that he had The Melody Room gig cemented for early February. I excitedly thanked him, told Earla, and drove down to Redondo Beach to tell Chet the good news. Chet was really happy, and for more reasons than one. He was happy he'd be playing before a live jazz audience, happy because he would prove the naysayers wrong. But he was happiest because he'd be able to start earning money to support his family. That, above all, was the most important to him. It was only going to be a three-night gig, but I felt very confident he could prove to the public and his fans that he could still play full sets in a jazz club. Then, I would make the rounds, like I'd promised, to try and get Chet signed to a recording contract.

About an hour and a half later, Chet and I were in a little drum shop in Hollywood on Sunset east of La Brea. The owner obviously knew who Chet was, and even though he was excited about Chet being in his store, he also seemed a little uptight. I couldn't figure out why.

The owner had just concluded business with a man and his son, thanking them as they walked out of the shop. The store was now empty, and the owner, curious to know why Chet was there, asked what he could do for him. Chet told the guy about his gig at The Melody Room and that his drummer, me, didn't have a set of drums, and would he be willing to let me have a set, and pay him later? The owner said he'd like to help but couldn't, because business had been slow and there was no way he could afford to let any drums go out of his place for less than two hundred and fifty bucks cash, and that was without cymbals and stands. Chet looked a bit downhearted and discouraged and thanked the man anyway.

As we were leaving, I thought of a friend, Gene Denacola, who was in Hollywood visiting his cousin, Nicky Blair. We had become very good friends as he was a drummer himself, and also very kind. If anyone would help me, it would be Gene. I called him, told him my story, and within the hour, he'd bought me a set of drums. I didn't need any cymbals or stands because I had my own original hand hammered Zildjian K cymbals from Istanbul, which I'd had since the mid 50's. I wouldn't have parted with those for love nor money. I still have them to this day.

With the drum issue settled, I wanted Chet to know how happy and excited I was about being on the stand as his drummer, and how I'd try my hardest to play with sensitivity behind him. When we got to my house, Chet helped me bring the drums inside and helped me set them up. I set up the two cymbal stands with my18 inch ride cymbals and tried the set out. They had a nice sound but needed to be properly tuned. "I'll tune 'em up later," I said and got up from behind the set and thanked him again for the chance to play drums for his comeback. He backed away shyly and lowered his head a little.

That was another interesting trait about Chet. He had this shyness about receiving any kind of thanks, like he wasn't worthy. It was like the time I'd mentioned him winning first place in the Downbeat and Metronome polls, and how he'd fluffed the whole idea off by saying he didn't feel he deserved to get first place; that there were other players out there who he felt did.

Chet really did have this thing about himself and his greatness as a trumpet player. He couldn't bring himself to believe that he was really as great as most of the critics and musicians were saying he was. And because of these feelings of self-doubt, he always felt he had to work harder and harder to achieve the sound and tone that would be his alone and would be recognized forever.

Chapter 20
Nothing Came Easy for Chet

There are a few critics and musicians out there who, for whatever reason, have made claims that Chet never had to work to become a great trumpeter, that everything just came to him naturally. Well, a part of that is true, especially the part of his talent having come to him as a gift from God. But everything else he had, he had to work his ass off to get. It was true that if you were fortunate enough to have seen him perform in person, that everything he played looked effortless. But believe me, it wasn't. Nothing ever came easy for Chet, even though it may have appeared that it had. I witnessed how much time, pain and effort it took out of him just to be able to play again, and play again he would!

The days leading up to the gig seemed to drag by. I guess it was because I was so anxious and excited over the prospect that I would soon be playing with my main inspiration in jazz. But not just on some regular type gig, but on his comeback gig. It was going to be an historic event and the thought of that heightened the excitement and anticipation of the event even more. I was all over the place. On the phone, calling reporters from the LA Times, the Herald and Variety, personal friends and musicians, informing them of the upcoming Chet Baker comeback gig. I spoke with jazz writer/composer/critic, Leonard Feather, prominent jazz disc jockeys like KBCA's Chuck Niles, also club owners and managers and record producers, asking each and every one of them to make it to The Melody Room on Friday night.

Every morning before leaving to work on the house I was painting, I'd spend a half hour to forty-five minutes on the phone. Whenever I had the time, I'd drive down to Redondo Beach to spend a little time with Chet and Carol. One time, when I arrived, Carol told me Chet was in the bathroom, playing into the linen closet. I went to the closed door to listen. Chet was practicing scales, broken thirds and melodies. That's pretty much all he'd do to build up his endurance and stamina. Carol let him know I was there and the three of us sat down and talked about his progress and the upcoming gig. Chet seemed ready but a little uneasy, whereas Carol seemed alive with hope. I felt strongly that her ever-constant encouragement, and my abiding faith in God, Jesus and the Holy Spirit, would soon bear fruit.

Another day, Chet dropped by my house. He had his horn with him and wanted to run through some tunes. We went into the den and started to play. After a couple of tunes he stopped and said he wanted to do some breathing exercises. I watched as Chet went through these strange exercises. He'd take in a long breath of air, hold it, take in another breath, without exhaling the first breath and hold it, then another and another never once exhaling, until he was unable to take in another breath of air. Then he'd very slowly let the air escape out of his mouth in short bursts and long, until there was nothing left to let out. Then he'd go through the whole breathing exercise thing again then play a couple tunes. The more I watched him the more excited and elated I became. Talk about a prayer being answered and a dream coming true. This was it! Chet was looking good, playing good and feeling good. Everything was good.

Chet had been practicing almost every day for hours. He even developed three different embouchures. This was truly amazing. The way a trumpet player uses the lips and tongue is the embouchure and Chet had developed three, one on the left side of his mouth, one on the right, and the one in the middle that was destroyed during the beating. This way, when he got tired with one, he could go to the second or the third.

For the next couple of days I busied myself covering every base about getting the word out on Chet's comeback taking place on the upcoming Friday night, now just three nights away. I continued to call the press, several movie stars, jazz musicians, critics and fans in general. I hadn't left a stone unturned. I even had my dearest mother flown out from Westbrook, Maine to spend a month or two with Earla, our kids and me. I wanted her to have the opportunity to see me play with Chet. My dad never had the opportunity to make a living playing his C melody sax. He died before he had the chance to see what he could have done. This was one of the reasons I really wanted my mother to share in my moment of being a part of Chet's comeback. So Earla and I made absolutely certain days before that we'd have a babysitter for the coming Friday night.

On Tuesday afternoon, three days before the gig, I got a phone call from Chet's mother. She was all stressed out about Chet. I asked her what he had done and she related that he'd been in a lot of pain the day before and had pawned his horn to buy food for the kids and medicine for himself. Vera felt bad because she didn't have enough money to buy him another trumpet, and he didn't know what he was going to do.

I couldn't believe my ears, but promised her I'd see what I could do about getting his horn back. Earla, who was busy putting the finishing stitches on the dress she was designing for my mother to wear at the Melody Room, overheard my part of the conversation and wanted to know what happened. I told her about Chet's situation and she didn't seem a bit surprised. Chet was no doubt very uptight about playing in front of a large audience again after such a lengthy period of time, and by pawning his horn, had probably given himself the perfect excuse not to play.

At first, I thought she was nuts. But the more I thought about it, the more plausible it became. I left the house and drove down to see Chet to check it out for myself. What Earla had said continued to dominate my thoughts, because she did have this special kind of intuition.

By the time I got to Chet's house, I was not only concerned, but also very discouraged. I knocked on the door and Carol let me in. I didn't see Chet and asked her where he was. She said he was in the bathroom and would be right out. I asked her if it were true that Chet had hocked his horn, and before she could answer, he came into the living room with a pained look in his eyes. I didn't want to hurt Chet's feelings any more than they had been during the last year and a half by displaying anger and criticism for what he had done. Instead, I wanted to prove that I cared by showing understanding.

"Well..." he began, with that long Chet Baker pause. "I was

in a lot of pain Art, and needed something bad, but didn't have the bread to get it so… I had to let the horn go."

"But why didn't you call me, Chet? You know I would have helped you somehow, man! What are we going to do? I've been calling everybody I can think of to tell them to make sure they make it up to the Melody Room to see you," I said. "And I know the place is going to be packed." I asked where he had hocked the horn and for how much.

He said he had pawned it with the same guy for a hundred bucks. When I heard that I was furious. "Oh man. If he gave you a hundred, there's no friggin' way he's going to give it back to me for less than two hundred! And there's no way I can come up with that kind of bread right now," I said. "That guy's a heartless prick, man! Can you think of anyone you might be able to borrow a trumpet from before Friday, man?"

He looked at me with pained eyes for a few seconds and spoke softly. "Well I can probably get one from Herb. I'm sure he has more than one."

"Herb Alpert?" I asked.

"Yeah," he said quietly. "I'll give him a call later today. I'm sure I'll have one by tomorrow." He said this with a casualness that just didn't seem right. There was something troubling him… something going on inside he wasn't telling me about.

"What's really happening, man? I've seen you go through pain before, but you didn't hock your horn just to buy pain pills."

"Well… I…" He paused for a few seconds then continued. "I'm a little nervous about facing an audience again after so long, you know? Wondering if there's even anyone really going to be showing up to hear me, and if they do, if they'd accept me back, or just walk out, you know?"

"Listen to me, man. You're CHET BAKER! And before you lost your teeth, you were considered the greatest lyrical trumpet player of all time!! This is your comeback, man, and you ARE ready!" I said. "This is your moment to re-establish yourself as the greatest lyrical player of all time," I said emphatically. "Just make sure you call Herb and get that trumpet."

He promised he would, and that was all I needed to know. I gave him a warm hug and left, confident with my faith in God that He would see to it that everything would work out fine.

I decided to take the long way home, stopping at the oil pumping machines along upper La Brea. It was sort of mesmerizing to sit there alongside the road watching these huge machines bobbing up and down constantly, looking like giant rocking horses digging for food.

I didn't know what it was, but the more I watched those machines the more it seemed like an exercise in futility. Like if the steel wire cord that pulled the chicken-like neck up and down suddenly broke, the whole machine would become immobile. Like Chet and his career. Thinking about that gave me a feeling of deep compassion for Chet, and it truly bothered me to think that a guy of Chet's world-wide fame and stature could actually be nervous about playing in front of a live audience in a packed club.

However, the longer I thought about it, the more I began to see and understand how and why he felt the way he did. All the many days, weeks, months and long hours of practice and physical and emotional pain he'd endured in order to re-develop his embouchure – everything he had worked for was at stake. He had been humiliated, maligned and ignored by those he thought were his friends. Club owners, club managers, record producers and musicians had turned their backs to him. And three nights from this day, he would be making his comeback performance.

If he failed in any way, his career as a trumpet player could be over then and there. On Friday night he'd be laying it all out for the people to see and hear. His heart, soul and future were being put on the line and all I could do was wait, hope and pray that he'd make it through that night; and that everyone in the club would enjoy his music and welcome him back with, if not with open arms, at least with appreciation for all he had to overcome to be back on the stand again. I said a long, fervent prayer and then drove home.

Chapter 21
Complications

I didn't sleep more than an hour the night before the gig because I was just too damn excited about the whole thing. So I got out of bed around 6:00am and made myself a cup of instant coffee, lit a cigarette, flicked the TV on to the morning news until my mother heard it and got up, quickly followed by Earla and the kids. I made breakfast for the bunch of us – scrambled eggs and pancakes. After the kids had their breakfast, I sent the two oldest ones off to school. I lit up another cigarette and held it in the corner of my mouth and played drums with my fingers on the counter top. It seemed I had a habit of doing that whenever I got nervous and my mother picked right up on it.

"What's the matter Arthur? Are you worried about playing with Chet tonight?"

"Well, yeah, in a way I guess I am. You know Momma, tonight's gonna to be the most important night of my life! If I still had my old tape recorder I'd be able to record the whole thing, you know?"

"Why don't you go to the Culver City pawn shop, Art?" Earla suggested. "You'd probably be able to pick up a used one there real cheap. At least it's worth a try."

She was right. I hadn't even thought about that. I left the house and drove to the pawnshop. Almost as soon as I entered the store, the manager came from behind the glass-enclosed counter and asked if he could help. I told him I was looking for a good tape recorder, but that I didn't want to pay and arm and a leg for it. He told me that he might have just what I was looking for and lead me to another area in the rear of the store. There he showed me a four track stereo tape recorder, which included a foot high directional microphone. I asked him what he wanted for it and when he told he had to get a hundred and fifty dollars, my heart sank because I didn't have that kind of money on me, and I really wanted to get it.

I emptied my pockets and put what money I had on the counter. I had exactly eighty-two dollars and change. I told the guy how important it was to me because I was going to be playing with the great jazz trumpet immortal Chet Baker, and wanted to tape it so I'd have a permanent record of those nights.

Well, much to my surprise and joy, he happened to be a fan of Chet's and said he'd let me have the recorder for seventy five bucks if I'd introduce him and his wife to Chet when they came to the club. Of course I would I told him and he gave me three reels of tape and a take up reel to boot. I thanked him and rushed home to set it up to learn the ins and outs of how it worked by recording of Earla and my mother doing skits. The recorder worked beautifully.

Later that afternoon around 5:00 pm, I had supper with Earla, my mother and the kids. I decided to leave a little early to go to Chet's house and make sure he was okay. He'd been acting a bit anxious the past few days, and I was concerned. This was probably going to be the most important night of my life, and more important, the beginning of a whole new life and career for Chet.

Everything had been working out wonderfully well for me. My first cousin, Philip 'Bunky" Buotte and his wife Lorraine would be watching our kids and also allowing Earla to use their car to take her and my mother to The Melody Room. This freed me to go down to Redondo Beach to pick Chet up and drive him to the club and have enough time left for him to greet his fans and pick out the tunes for our first set.

I left the house about 6:00 pm, and man, was it raining! Each drop felt like the weight of a quarter when it hit my head. I was worried the rain might well discourage people from coming out to Chet's opening. I jumped into my car and took off for Redondo Beach.

The roads were slick and dark, and the wipers were barely able to keep the windshield clear of the rapidly falling rain. I took my time and arrived at Chet's house around 6:40 pm. I knocked on the door and a few seconds later the door opened and there stood Carol with a look of concern written across her beautiful face.

"What's the matter?" I asked.

Carol invited me in and quickly closed the door. I looked around and saw the three kids seated at the kitchen table eating supper, and noticed a trumpet case on the couch, but no Chet.

"Where's Chet, Carol?" I asked nervously.

Apparently, Chet had gone to the store to get some cigarettes and a half gallon of milk. She hoped he'd be coming back shortly. The kids had finished eating and Carol told them to go upstairs to bed. Without argument or fuss, the three of them quickly obeyed, kissed her on the cheek said goodnight to the two of us and disappeared up the stairs.

"Where'd he get the trumpet," I asked.

She said he'd gotten it from Herb Alpert and had already tried it out, so everything seemed to be okay.

I was relieved he had a trumpet, but was real concerned that he wasn't home. "How long has he been gone?" She figured maybe a half hour.

I looked at my wristwatch. It was getting close to 7 pm and that made me very nervous. She fixed a cup of hot tea. With each sip of tea she drank, I glanced at my watch. Another ten minutes had passed by and still no Chet. Now I was really anxious. I looked toward the door and back to her, punching my hand with my fist nervously.

"Where the hell is he, why isn't he here?!" I asked growing edgier by the second. "It's a good thing I went to the club this afternoon to set my drums up, otherwise…" I stopped and let the thought die. "Man, he knows how frigging hard I've worked to set this whole thing up. If he doesn't make THIS gig, he'll probably NEVER get another one in L.A.!!!!"

She realized that and was really hoping Chet would return home soon.

"This could very possibly be the single most important night of his life, and maybe even his future. And he's not even here."

I was actually more worried than I was angry because I truly did want to see him working again more than anything else.

Carol got up off the sofa, walked to the front door, opened it and looked out at the rainy, pitch black for a few seconds then closed the door. She walked back to the kitchen, lit up a cigarette and made herself another cup of tea, doing her very best to cover the fear and anxiety she was beginning to feel.

I glanced at my watch again. It was going on 7:15 pm.

"You think he would have gone to his mother's house for any reason?" I asked. "Would he have gone anywhere else after going to the store, maybe having the neighbor take him someplace afterwards?"

She shrugged nervously and said she couldn't think of any other place but the variety store up the street.

"What about that guy, what's his name, the guy who works in a bakery around here? You know the one I mean? You think he could be there?"

She looked surprised that she hadn't thought about it before and said that Chet could very well be with his friend, Norman, at the bakery.

"Where's this bakery located, and what's this Norman cat like?"

She told me Norman was a pretty nice man and may have been a one-time addict. Chet would sometimes drop in to see him and the two would share a little grass together. She felt it would be a good idea for me to check the bakery out to see if Chet was there.

I asked her for directions, and as soon as she had written them down, I grabbed the paper and immediately left the house. I had no trouble at all finding it. And when I went inside, there was Chet lying in a semi-fetal position, sound asleep on top of five or six 100 lbs. bags of flour. Norman was the only other person in the place. I told him who I was and why I was there and how important it was for me to get Chet back to his house, cleaned up and to the club in Hollywood all before 9 o'clock.

Norman was very understanding and helped me get the sleeping Chet out into my car where he continued to sleep with his head resting on the dashboard. His hair, clothes and shoes were covered with white flour, and I had all I could do to keep myself from laughing and crying at the same time. Before I closed the car door I had to know what I was dealing with.

"Tell me the truth, Norman. Did you give Chet any heroin?" He assured me emphatically that he hadn't given Chet any kind of drug. He swore that when Chet came into the bakery he looked like he had just copped and was looking for a safe place to sleep it off. That was all he knew. I thanked him for helping me and drove back to Chet's house.

When I pulled up in front of the house Carol was standing at the open door waiting. As soon as she saw my car pull up, she ran out through the rain and opened the passenger side door. Chet, his head resting against the dashboard, was still half-asleep.

"I pray to God he hasn't taken any of that heroin shit. That's all we'd need," I said.

Carol leaned further inside the car and placed her arm around his shoulder, asking Chet what he had taken.

He mumbled something but I really couldn't make it out. Carol reached under his chin and tilted his face up. He mumbled something again. She placed her ear close to his mouth and he half whispered, half mumbled again.

"What'd he say?"

She looked at me and shrugged.

"Sounded like he said sleeping pills." I looked at him again. "He's gotta be on something stronger than that, don't you think? Could he have taken heroin?

Carol, ever hopeful, felt that he could very well have taken a number of sleeping pills and have somewhat the same reaction.

I was thinking to myself that she could very well be right, giving her the benefit of doubt. After all, she'd probably seen him like this a few times before and knew far better than I did. Still, I had my doubts. But I sure as hell wasn't going to dampen the hope she held that he was kicking heroin for her and their children's sake because she had been doing everything humanly possible a loyal and loving wife could do to take care of him.

"Well we'd better hurry up and get him out of here," I said. I got out and ran around to the passenger side to help Carol lift him up out of the car, and between the two of us, we walked him inside the house out of the rain. "If we get him cleaned up fast enough, I'll be able to get us to the club on time."

Once we had him inside, I couldn't help but notice that Carol had been soaked to the bone with both her clothes and hair clinging tightly like glue.

"Oh, Carol. Look at your clothes, they're ruined."

She gave herself a quick once over and shrugged like it didn't really matter and asked me to help her. We lifted Chet off the couch and got him into the bathroom just off the kitchen so she could give him a bath. I left as she started to remove his wet clothes and stood just outside the closed door in case she needed me to assist her. I listened as she turned on the faucets. After a while, I could hear him tell her that he was all right and wanted to get up out of the tub. She told him to hold onto her while she helped him out, and a few seconds later, she opened the door. There was Chet wrapped with a big towel, still soaking wet. Carol and I walked him into the living room and gently seated him on the couch. We were both thankful that the kids had not witnessed their father in that condition, having already gone upstairs to bed a half hour earlier.

He was still in a semi-conscious state so Carol asked me to sit on the couch with him while she went upstairs to their bedroom to get him some clothes. She was up and back in a matter of seconds and the two of us sat on either side of Chet and between the two of us got him dressed. Carol patiently combed his hair and soon he was all ready to go. It was so vividly clear how deeply she loved and cared for Chet.

We got him into the car. I locked the door and walked Carol back into the house. I was very moved by her loving patience and understanding. I confided in her that Chet had often mentioned to me how much he really loved and needed her and how he had said that without her and the kids, he'd be nothing. I had just seen, firsthand, why. A happy smile illumined her face. I gave her a warm hug.

"I sure hope he comes out of it before we reach the club, Carol."

She was very confident that once I got Chet into the club, he'd come out of it and be ready to play. I believed her because she knew Chet better than anyone on earth. I smiled, gave her another hug and ran back to the car and got in, hoping she was right. I waved to her and then drove off into the pouring rain.

In those days we didn't have seat belts, and as soon as the car started moving, Chet's body lurched forward causing his head to fall on his knees and his shoulders and arms to hang dead-like on either side with both hands on the floorboard.

The rain didn't seem to be letting up at all. If anything, it was coming down stronger. Surprisingly, the traffic wasn't slowing down either. I glanced over at Chet and couldn't help but feel sorrow for him. Each time I checked on him I kept wondering how much longer it was going to be before he snapped out of it and came to his senses. I had to wake him up. I had to find a way to get him up and going soon.

"CHET! CHET! WAKE UP, MAN!!!!" He didn't respond at all so I tried again, this time I reached over and shook him roughly. "CHET!! WAKE UP!! You want a cigarette man?"

Finally, he made a moaning sound, slowly lifted his head and turned toward me.

"Yeah man, thanks," he said. I lit up a cigarette and passed it down to him. He raised his head up, looked at me and smiled, took a long drag, exhaled the smoke, then his body leaned forward again and his hands fell back down to the floorboard, only this time, his left hand was holding a burning cigarette in it. Without warning, some kind of foreign sports car raced by us in the driving rain and pulled directly in front of me, causing me to swerve dangerously off to the side of the road. But I had to keep going because of the traffic behind me. I yelled out something to the driver, looked down to check on Chet and noticed that the cigarette he was holding was actually burning between his fingers.

I immediately started looking for the first roadside rest area to pull over into and found one around the next bend. I quickly pulled over, parked and ran around to the passenger side door, opened it and helped him to sit upright, then took the cigarette out of his hand and flicked it into the falling rain. I shook his shoulder until he opened his eyes, and asked if he were all right. I felt so bad for him.

"Oh Chet… you burned your fingers, man. Oh man, you all right Chet?" He lifted both hands and regarded each one curiously and noticed the two fingers of his left hand had been burned. He didn't act like it had given him any pain.

"Well… I don't really feel anything, man… so it must be alright." And with that, he leaned back against the seat, closed his eyes. That had to have really hurt him. But if it had, he sure as hell wasn't showing it. I still couldn't help but feel pain in my heart for him. However, I did feel more comfortable about one thing – the fact that he was now seated in an upright position.

I got back into the car and drove off, making sure not to make any unnecessary sharp turns along the way that would result in launching him forward against the dash. I glanced at my watch. It was approximately 8:35 pm. I figured I still had enough time to make it to the club on time. I looked at Chet again and asked how he was doing; all the while hoping that he'd finally show signs of coming out of it and would be in condition to play at least a little.

"How are you feeling now, Chet? Are you going to be alright, man?" I asked.

"Yeah... yeah, I'll be alright, man..." he said wearily, then laid his head back against the seat again and closed his eyes. And then, out of the blue, he asked, "Where are we now, Art?"

"LaCienega, and Sunset. We should be at the club in a few minutes," I replied.

I came to Sunset Boulevard and hung a left and drove west along Sunset until I reached the underground parking building across from The Classic Cat Strip Club and The Melody Room, quickly found a spot and parked the car. I got out and helped Chet because he was still a little weak and a bit unsteady on his feet. I held him against the car, reached in, grabbed his trumpet case and shut the door. I stood there with him until he was strong enough to walk under his own power. We walked to the opening of the building where we could look out and see Sunset Boulevard and directly across the street, see both The Classic Cat and The Melody Room.

It was then that I noticed that the C in Chet's first name was missing. The marquee read, "HET BAKER & FRIENDS." I didn't let on at that point, hoping he wouldn't notice it. We stood there for another few seconds. I asked him if he wanted another cigarette. He just nodded, so I lit one up for him and one for myself. He took a couple of drags, exhaled, and looked around curiously, then closed his eyes. I was concerned because he didn't seem to be coming out of it fast enough. Maybe he had taken sleeping pills after all. I wasn't sure. I just believed what Carol had told me about his always managing to find a way to snap out of it and be able to play.

"C'mon Chet.... we're here now."

He opened his eyes, looked at me, then past me and back to me again curiously. "Where's here?"

"The Melody Room! Over there across the street," I said, pointing to the marquee. "That's where we're playing tonight, man." He looked across Sunset to the club and recognized it. "You're gonna be able to make it, aren't you Chet? Everybody's waiting to see you, man. Just like we hoped they would."

He nodded slowly and looked up to the marquee and noticed the missing letter from his first name. Pissed, he said, "Look at that shit, man. They couldn't even spell my fuckin' name right."

"The rain must have knocked the C down," I said. "It doesn't matter anyway, man. Everybody knows it's you."

He sighed and looked at me through half opened eyes. I'm thinking to myself, there's no way he's going to be able to make it across Sunset, let alone play. I didn't know what kind of drug he'd taken, or the exact amount, but whatever it was, it sure as hell wasn't wearing off fast enough. I felt the best thing to do, was to get him to walk.

So we made our way out of the underground parking lot on to Sunset Boulevard, and from there into the crosswalk. It was at the crosswalk that he started coming out of his fog and within moments, was fully aware again.

We started across, but we must have been crossing on a green light, because the cars were whizzing by, blowing their horns and very nearly hitting us. By the time we reached the halfway point, the two of us had nearly been struck several times. I decided it would be safer for us to stay where we were until the traffic light changed.

Once clear, we crossed and stood on the corner of Sunset and Larrabee. On the east side of us was The Classic Cat strip club, and a short distance from where we stood to the west, was a pharmacy. Next to it was The Melody Room. I could see people opening the door and going inside. Just then Earla came through the door. She spotted us and came over immediately. She was excited and told Chet the place was packed, and everyone was waiting inside to see him. He managed a weak smile and acknowledged her with a weary nod of the head.

I told Earla to go inside the club and tell the piano player, Frank Strazzeri, one of the finest bop piano players in the world, that we were just outside and would be coming in a few minutes. She agreed, left us and went into the club.

"You hear what she said, man? The place is packed and they're all waiting to see and hear you play again. Isn't it great, man?" He nodded and said something about our getting out of the rain because we were getting drenched.

My mind had become so concerned with getting Chet to straighten out that I had become almost oblivious to the rain. I wanted to give him a couple more minutes before going in, so we walked into the alcove of the drugstore and stood there watching the rain slapping the pavement as though it wanted to punch its way through the cement. Unconsciously Chet reached into his back pocket and came out with a comb and slicked his wet hair back then handed the comb to me. I did likewise. He looked off into the moving traffic along Sunset Blvd. for a few moments. When he looked back at me it was evident that something was weighing on his mind. Looking at him standing there I wasn't a hundred percent sure how he was actually feeling about wanting to go into the club and play.

"Listen, Chet. I love you, man. But if you feel that you're really not up to playing... if you're still feeling too sick... then forget about it, man, you don't have to do it. I mean it. We'll just find some other club somewhere, sometime." I placed my hand on his shoulder. "I don't think there's anything else I can do, Chet. It's your life. It's up to you now, man." He blinked his eyes a couple times, looked at me and smiled that boyish Chet Baker grin, but didn't speak a word.

"Are you afraid, Chet?" I asked quietly, but he didn't answer. "You are, aren't you, man? You really don't wanna go into the club do you?"

He looked off into the falling rain like he wanted to avoid the question, then turned back to me. He was nervous. No, he was more than just nervous. He was worried – worried whether or not he still had what it took to play, even after all the hours, days, weeks and months of arduous and often painful practice, and maybe scared for precisely the same reason.

"Well... I'm always a little nervous... it's always given me an edge. But tonight... well... we'll have to wait and see," he said in his soft voice.

"Everything's gonna be cool, Chet. I can feel it." I was confident, but Chet expressed a concern about the possibility of his not being able to measure up to what he once was.

"Measure up??!!" I shot back. "Man, as soon as you blow that first note, the world will know that you're back, baby! I can't imagine how nervous you are... But you've got to remember WHO you are, man. You're known the world over! Listen to me, Chet. This is your comeback performance! This is what you've been working for. You gotta go in this place and show these people that you beat the odds and that you're back!" I said with heartfelt conviction. "C'mon Chet... Let's go in there and play our asses off!" Then a moment took place that I'll never forget. Chet looked at me for a few seconds with this intense looking stare, and in his eyes I could see the pain, fear and concern. He inhaled deeply and exhaled into a long deep sigh as though he had reached a conclusion. Another moment passed and took the trumpet case out of my hand and into his.

"I'm ready, Art. Let's go in and re-gather our chops together, man," he said intently.

And with that simple statement, the two of us opened the door to The Melody Room and walked into history.

Chapter 22
Comeback at the Melody Room

"His (Chet's) first professional appearance was at the Melody Room in Hollywood (soon to be released on CCB label). A fellow musician and longtime friend, Artt Frank, had become acquainted with Chet during his struggle to play again ... It was Artt that arranged the Melody Room engagement, which, by the way, Chet and Artt taped that night just to see how bad he sounded."

Carol Baker
(Quarterly Magazine
"Chet's Choice")

Chet and I opened the door and walked into the club. A busy champagne & hors d'oeuvres party was in progress, apparently set up by Hal Cohn for Chet's comeback performance celebration. As soon as Chet walked into the club, an immediate hush fell upon the room. Every eye focused on Chet because he looked tired and a bit wasted. As we made our way over to the bar, Hal came out of the crowd to greet us and take Chet over to meet Tony, the owner of the club. As we made our way, I could hear the whispering of the doubters and backbiters saying, "Look at him, he can hardly walk." And then another man whispered, "He's wet and strung out. There's no way he's going to be able to play." And I suppose from their perspective, and their lack of knowledge of Chet's inner strength and desire, I probably would have felt the same way as they did.

We reached Tony at the end of the bar and Hal introduced Chet to him. Tony was a short Greek man, and when he spoke, he reminded me of the little Caesar character once portrayed by Edward G. Robinson. He didn't know a damn thing about jazz, and didn't have the slightest idea who Chet was. He didn't even care about meeting him; all he seemed to care about was filling the glasses with beer and whiskey. He didn't care about the party going on; he just wanted to know when we were going to play. "We're going up to the stand right now, Tony. We'll be starting in a few minutes, OK?"

"Yeah, alright, just get up there and play," he answered. Hal gestured and told us not to worry about Tony, that he was more bark than bite. Earla came over and suggested that Chet and I remove our wet suit coats so it would be easier for us to play. We did and gave them to her and she went back to her table. We left Hal and made our way over to the bandstand, literally having to push our way through some of the people who were still filling their faces with food and drink.

The interior of The Melody Room had a dark and mysterious feel to it. The ceiling was black with red psychedelic lights flashing all over the room, giving the place an unmistakable rock joint atmosphere. It was, for sure, a very bizarre looking place for a man of Chet's stature to be making his comeback, but we were both thankful that he at least had some place to do it!

Every seat along the bar was taken, as was every booth. A horseshoe bar surrounded the bandstand, and every seat around that was likewise taken. Chet, still being a little weak and unsure, made his way up to the bandstand. I joined him and we greeted the two musicians who had been there waiting patiently for us. Frank Strazzeri, the piano player, had worked with Chet on several occasions before this night. He was not only a lyrical player, but also a swinging bop player. David Dyson was a great bassist and had played with the likes of Phil Moore III and organist, Earl Grant. Chet went to a chair directly in front of the drum set, seated himself wearily and closed his eyes.

Due to the limited amount of space on the stand, I had been forced to set the drums up with my back right up against the rear portion of the horseshoe bar. It would prove to be a blessing for me because I was able to set up the tape recorder on the bar area right behind me and control every facet of whatever I wanted to record. I walked over to Chet, bent down next to his ear and asked him if he was all right. He opened his eyes and smiled. "Yeah, I'm cool, man." I told him I was going to get my tape recorder and he told me to hurry because we'd be starting in a few minutes. I left the stand, the club, ran across to the car, grabbed the recorder, came back and had it all set up and ready to go within two minutes. Chet was still seated in the chair; head bent forward, a bit weary, and completely oblivious to the murmurings of the people in the club. I was really sweating it, wondering, worrying if in fact Chet was really going to be able to play, or if he was going to fall flat on his face. I just didn't know.

From my vantage point behind the drums, I was able to look around. There were many famous people in the room, movie stars of the time Frankie Avalon, Michael Dante, Angel Tompkins, and Earl Holliman. Also present were restaurateur Nicky Blair, Carole Curb, sister of Mike Curb, singer/composer and movie producer, Herb Alpert, Sally Bruce, mother of famed comic, Lenny Bruce, and Lenny's widow, Honey Bruce, jazz radio announcer Chuck Niles, and Ike and Tina Turner, plus many other well-known jazz musicians, fans, and friends.

Chet continued to sit there in the chair motionless except for nervously biting his lower lip. Then he opened his eyes, leaned forward a few inches and told Frank Strazzeri he wanted to open with *Fair Weather*. As soon as he had spoken, a death-like silence filled the air. It was un-nerving to say the least. He turned and looked at me over his right shoulder.

"I leave a lot of spaces, Art. Just fill the spaces."

What he said there is something I shall never, ever forget for as long as I live and play drums. In fact, I continue to give this very same advice to every drummer I've ever given lessons to or coached.

Chet brought the horn up to his mouth, counted off the time, and began to play. Every pair of eyes in that club were riveted on him. He played tentative at first, blowing only short phrases throughout the chorus. But that pure, especially haunting, unmistakable sound that was Chet's alone was still there and being heard anew.

Everything seemed like magic. He was playing again, and I couldn't have been happier just to be there on this night of nights playing drums with him. Adding to the magic of it all for me was the most precious and important person, my beloved mother Rose Ann Frank, present with my wife, to witness it as well. It was an unbelievable sensation to say the least.

When Chet took his first solo, I held my breath and prayed that he would not falter or make any mistakes, and thank God above, he didn't. He played beautifully and it was wonderful to say the least. His tone was rich, fat and warm. And though he played sparingly what he did play was beautiful.

When he ended his solo, the room exploded into an almost ear deafening applause, yelling and whistling. I really can't begin to put into words the way I felt at that moment in time, so proud and exhilarated. So overjoyed and blessed to have just been a part of jazz history. God had answered my prayers. Chet was back, and here I was, in Hollywood, California, on the stand with the great Chet Baker. It could never get any better than this.

While the applause continued, Chet turned and looked over his shoulder to me with a look of pain etched over his face. He gestured that his bridge was giving him trouble, then turned and lowered the trumpet to his knee and rested his chin on his hand while Frank played his solo. David Dyson then took a beautiful bass solo, after which Chet brought the horn back to his mouth and brought the tune to an end. Again the place erupted with thunderous applause lasting nearly two minutes. I reached over and squeezed Chet on the shoulder. "Is the frigging bridge bothering you again, Chet?"

He turned and looked over his shoulder at me again with a sigh of dismay.

"Yeah… it keeps popping loose and I have to use all my strength just to keep that fucking mouthpiece up against my mouth." He was visibly shaken by the ordeal but managed to maintain his composure. He leaned forward to Frank Strazzeri. "Frank, you, Art and Dave do a trio thing while I go to the head and put some glue on this bastard."

He got up and left the stand, and as soon as he did, I could hear the murmuring of some of the people in the audience. Some whispering within my ear range felt he was going into the bathroom to get a fix. Little did these people know the great difficulty Chet had with his false teeth. The audience had no idea what the man had to endure just to be able to play again. Whenever he left the stand in the middle of a set or directly after, people invariably always drew the wrong conclusions.

Frank Strazzeri called a medium up-tempo tune and we played until Chet came back on to the stand, seated himself, took his horn and joined us, much to the delight of the crowd. When the tune ended, we received a nice round of applause. I reached out and tapped Chet on the shoulder happily, and said, "They love you, man. They love ya."

We finished our first set and came down off the stage, into the audience. The first people we met were Ike and Tina Turner, followed by Michael Dante, Frankie Avalon and Earl Holliman. A bit later, Chet and I were on our way outside to have a smoke when we heard someone call out to him. We turned around and Herb Alpert was coming toward us. He had a warm smile and his right hand extended to Chet. "So good to hear you play again. You still sound so beautiful." Chet smiled, thanked him and introduced me to Herb. He shook my hand, and asked us to join him at his table. Chet and I followed him to his table. We sat across from him and a beautiful young lady. Herb asked us if we wanted a drink and we both ordered a bottle of beer.

I didn't know anything about the personal side of Herb, but knew when somebody had something on their mind. He asked Chet if everything was all right with the trumpet, were the valves working properly, did he have enough valve oil and things like that. It seemed as if Herb wanted to talk to Chet about more important things, but wasn't quite sure how or where to begin. He told Chet that he had known all about what he'd been going through the last couple of years. When Chet called to borrow a trumpet, Herb hadn't had the chance to tell Chet that whatever he needed, all he'd have to do was to ask.

Chet lowered his head to the table for a second then looked up at Herb. "Thanks, man," he said, stopped and lowered his head again.

"Listen," Herb said, and reached his hand across the table and placed it on Chet's arm. "If you'd let me, Chet, I'd like to help you out a little financially." He placed his right hand over his heart. "Please don't take it as an insult, Chet. You're a great player, and I'd just like to help."

Chet was visibly moved and thanked Herb for the thought. "I don't know how or when I'd be able to repay you, Herb. This is the first real gig I've had in months, and I don't know when I'll be getting another, you know."

"Tell you what, Chet. Could you teach me how to improvise? I'd be more than happy to pay for the lessons. That way, we'd both be getting something out of it. What do you say?"

Chet was perplexed. "Teach you how to improvise? I can't teach you how to improvise, Herb. Improvisation is governed by your imagination or lack thereof!"

Herb, being a trumpet player himself, knew full well that improvisation was not something that could be taught. One either had the ability to do so or one did not. I could see what Herb was trying to do, however. He knew Chet's personal situation and was doing his best to find an honorable way to give Chet a helping hand without causing him any kind of embarrassment.

Not really knowing anything about a trumpet myself, and not wanting Chet to miss out on the chance of being able to earn some money, I decided to make a quick suggestion.

"You could probably teach him what you were showing me at my house, Chet. You know, when you were doing all that, going up and down the scale slowly stuff, using those thirds, and doubling up… Something like that."

Chet thought about it for a few seconds then related to Herb that he would be willing to try to teach him whatever he could, which made Herb very happy. He asked Chet to come to his studio on the following Monday afternoon and extended the invitation for me to come along also. Chet and I exchanged looks and agreed.

I had a strong feeling that Herb was the kind of guy who was genuinely interested in helping Chet in any way he could, which made me very happy.

Just about that time I saw Frank Strazzeri go up onto the stand and sit at the piano, followed by David Dyson. I nudged Chet and told him that Frank and David were on the stand waiting for us. He turned, looked over, then back to Herb and asked him if there was anything particular he wanted to hear. Herb told him he'd like to hear, *My Funny Valentine*. Chet acknowledged the request and we made our way up to the bandstand to join the other two musicians.

As soon as we sat down, the place grew quiet again. Chet called out, *On Green Dolphin Street* to begin the second set, and man, his solo was fantastic! With each tune he played, his chops grew stronger, as did his self-confidence. Chet called a Miles Davis tune called, *Solar*, and stretched out a little more on this one. The next tune we did was a blues tune called, *Blue 'n' Boogie*. And again, Chet had found the old fire within and was cookin'! When this tune ended he received rousing applause.

The next tune we did was Herb's request, *My Funny Valentine*. Before we played it, Chet turned to me and was very specific about how fast he wanted the tempo set, and he wanted it slow. And slow he played it, singing the first chorus with the plaintiveness of a man who'd lost a love and wanted desperately for his '*little Valentine to stay and make each day Valentine's day,*' then lifted his trumpet and played a beautiful, lyrically haunting solo, followed by a wonderful piano solo from Frank, with Chet picking up the thread and taking the tune to a conclusion. The applause was deafening and brought a big smile to our faces. Chet turned to one side and started rubbing the side of his cheek and jaw, and I knew immediately that he was hurting.

"Are you going to be alright Chet…?" I asked with concern.

"Well, I'm starting to hurt little, Art," he said and ran a hand over his cheek and mouth again.

"You got anything on you, you can take?"

"Yeah, I gotta a couple of pain pills I can take," he said softly.

"Well, take them if it'll help you, man," I said in hopes they would. He excused himself and left the stand and went to the bar to get a glass of water, reached into his pants pocket and withdrew a small bottle of pills just as I walked up and stood beside him. He opened the bottle and removed two pills, placed them in his mouth and took a drink of water. "You think you'll be alright for the rest of the night, Chet?"

A long sigh, "Yeah, I should be alright now, Art. I should be alright now," he said, and looked at me with the saddest, pain-filled eyes I'd ever seen.

"I love ya, man. And I hope you make it all the way back to the top."

"Thanks, Art. I love you too, man, and appreciate all you're doing," he said. "C'mon. Let's go outside and have a smoke."

Outside the rain had stopped and the weather had turned fair, at least for moment. Chet and I lit up a cigarette and within a few seconds several fans came over to him to say hello and say how thrilled they were to see him and hear him play again. Other fans came over to ask for his autograph, which he was more than happy to do. As I stood by watching I couldn't help but feel thrilled for him because this was precisely what he needed. After a few more minutes, we excused ourselves from the people and made our way back inside the club. We still had another set to get through.

Once back on the stand Chet managed to play half of the next set through pain. However, once the pills took effect, he played with relative ease for the remainder of the set. We finished on an up tempo tune and he received a standing ovation. He so needed to hear the applause in his ears again. He so needed to know that he still had fans, still had people who liked his music, and would come out to support him. As the applause continued he turned, looked at me and smiled that special boyish smile that was his alone.

Once the applause faded out, Chet turned to me and asked if I'd mind if he asked Earla to come up to sing. I told him I thought it was a good idea. Chet really dug Earla's singing, and through the years, he would ask her to sing anytime she happened to be in a club where he was appearing. The break would also give him a chance to rest his chops a little. He reached for the microphone, tapped it a couple times to make sure it was on.

"We have a wonderful singer in the house tonight, and we'd like to invite her up to do a tune with us. Ladies and Gentlemen, the lovely Earla Frank!"

The audience erupted into applause as Earla, surprised, looked up at Chet, and me but didn't make a move. Chet spoke over the microphone again, "Come on up and sing for us Earla."

Another round of applause, and she rose up out of the booth and made her way up to the stand and over to Chet, who handed her the microphone. Frank Strazzeri asked her what tune she wanted to do. Just like jazz musicians who often carried their instruments with them when visiting a club, hoping to sit in, jazz singers in those days always carried their lead sheets, just in case they were invited to sing. Earla handed Frank the lead sheet of the music for *Angel Eyes*. Earla had a great voice (still does). She sounds a lot like a burry trombone, deep, rich and lyrically poignant.

Frank placed the sheet music on the piano so he and David

could look it over together. Satisfied, he told Earla they were ready and she snapped her fingers in a slow ballad tempo and began to sing. Her tone was full and she sang in a broad, breathy style, not too torchy, but with a poignant plaintiveness of lost love. In short, romantically cool.

Chet gave her his full attention, and when she brought the tune to an end, he immediately stood up and applauded; the entire audience quickly followed suit. Chet asked her to do another tune but she declined, telling us both later that she did not want to take anything away from his long awaited comeback performance. As Earla walked by the bar to get back to her booth, some big guy grabbed her by the arm and pulled her over to him. I immediately jumped up from behind my drums and ran down to the bar. He said something and tried to sucker punch me with his right hand but I ducked under his swing and was about to counter with a short right hook to his jaw, but changed my mind. Instead, I grabbed his arm and spun his body around until I had him in neck lock.

"That's my wife you just grabbed, pal! Don't ever put your fuckin' hands on her again, man, or next time I'll break every rib in your chest!!" I turned to the patrons at the bar. "You all saw what happened. He threw the first punch."

A couple nodded in agreement and the man himself apologized profusely, telling me how out of line he'd been. I let him go and he turned to me with his hand extended. I held no hard feelings for the guy and shook his hand. He told me he was recently divorced and when he heard Earla singing *Angel Eyes* it made him sad because the song reminded him of his wife. I told him I was sorry for losing my cool and wished him the best, then went back to the bandstand to join Chet and the others.

Chet kicked off a medium tempo tune called *Look for the Silver Lining*, after which we played a few more tunes then ended the set. The four of us came down off the stand and just about every person in the room immediately greeted Chet. I moved over to the bar to see if the man I'd confronted was still there. But he had apparently left during the last set. I couldn't help but feel sad for the guy. He was probably all alone in the world and I had come along and nearly broken his neck.

I moved over to join Earla and my mother, asking if she was

having a good time. Tears started to roll down over her cheeks. She reached out and held my hand, telling me how proud she was, and how proud my father would have been. I didn't know what to say or do, so I just bent down and hugged her. I lit up a cigarette and looked over to watch Chet. He had so much joy on his face. I was so happy for him. It felt so good to see him being wanted again.

Chet's comeback performance had been a success. I went around the horseshoe bar to the tape recorder, took off the reels and placed them in their boxes. As I was taking the recorder off of the counter Chet walked over and asked if I'd heard any of the night's taping. I hadn't and suggested he come by my house early the following evening on his way to the gig and we'd sit down and listen together.

Chapter 23
Keeping Time

Chet was at my house the following evening around 6:30 pm, and I had the tape all set up and ready to go. We sat at the table and listened to the first few tunes and agreed he had played a bit tentative, but lyrically beautiful. We listened to another tune, and then to his signature tune, *My Funny Valentine*. I wasn't at all happy at the way I was playing behind Chet. There was absolutely nothing wrong with my time or anything like that - it was more about 'how' and 'where' I was placing it. Chet was singing as he usually did, just a little behind the beat, and instead of me bringing it down to where he was laying his time, I continued to come down on the usual 'two/four thing' which to my ears, made the time sound forced.

"What am I doin' wrong there, Chet? Why does the time sound weird to me?"

He looked at me with a smile and nodded. "There's nothing wrong with your time, man. You were right there," he said firmly.

"Then why did it sound forced to me?" I asked.

"Well, playing drums on a laid back ballad requires a whole different range of dynamics, emotion and feeling. Most drummers tend to play on a ballad the same way they do on an uptempo thing. Playing a ballad is not just about keeping the time… it's much more than that. It's more about *feeling* the time than it is in just applying it. Keeping time behind the way I play a ballad should be more implied than directly stated. Expressing it rather than announcing it."

He asked if I understood. I didn't want to lie and make off like I was a know-it-all because if I did, I wouldn't be able to learn a thing. I really wanted to learn all I could from him, so I told him I wasn't really sure.

"Well... sometime later on I'll pick out a tune and show you what I mean."

It was time to leave for the club. Thank God, it wasn't raining. Once there, we were both quite surprised to see most of the same movie actors, actresses, musicians and radio personnel who'd been there the night before. As we went up onto the stand Chet gestured, waved and nodded to most of the people before walking over to say hello to pianist Frank Strazzeri. David Dyson, the bassist for last night had a previous gig and would not be making it with us tonight, so Chet had hired the great bassist, Frank De La Rosa for the next two nights. He was absolutely fantastic! Frank had been Ella Fitzgerald's bassist for quite a while and had also worked with many other name players. I sat behind my drums and waited for Chet to kick off the first tune, which he soon did, called *Here I'll Stay*, in a medium, bright tempo. I couldn't help but notice how much better Chet's playing was becoming. He was less tentative and was taking more chances, and soloing for two and three choruses instead of just one.

I also noticed the special way Chet had of keeping time. It was indeed very unusual. He'd sit with his left leg crossed over his right and on the first beat he would push his left toe toward the floor then snap it to the right, then to the left, then up, then down again similar to a conductor's arc. Strange, but for Chet, it worked perfectly.

After our first set ended, Chet was off talking to a couple of fans while I asked Frank Strazzeri what he thought of Chet's playing. "He's starting to play a little faster, isn't he?"

"Yeah, a couple more nights like this and we'll be the ones chasing him!" Strazzeri noted. "He's really starting to come on, man."

Frank didn't say a hell of a lot. But when he did, he knew what he was talking about. I turned and looked around the room and noticed Sally and Honey Bruce seated at the far end of the horseshoe bar. I went over to say hello to them. Sally talked a great deal about how much she missed Lenny, and how much Chet reminded her of him. Seeing him up close and talking with Chet caused her to feel a special closeness to him. Sally also told me she honestly felt that Chet and Lenny had a lot in common.

Lenny had been a drug addict and Chet was trying to overcome his addiction. And both men, as far as she was concerned, were geniuses. I totally agreed with her. I spent a few more minutes with them and left to go find Chet, who was still engaged in conversation. I gestured that I was going up to the bandstand to wait for the second set to start, but on the way, I spotted Tina Turner sitting at the other end of the horseshoe bar by herself and walked over to sit beside her. She had been here for a few minutes the night before and confided to me that she had thoroughly enjoyed his playing and my drumming. We talked for a few minutes more, until she had to leave and go across the street to work at the Classic Cat, where she and her husband, Ike, were the headline performers.

Tina invited Chet and me to come over to see her perform during our next break. I promised her that I'd see if I could get him to go. As it turned out, Chet very was agreeable to it, so we went over to watch Tina and were very impressed with her singing, magnetic personality and stage presence. It was clear that she would become the very famous performer she is today. We would have liked to have hung around but had to get back to the Melody Room.

At the start of our second set, more people were coming into the club and it looked like it was going to be another great night for playing. Though we had never met, I recognized the internationally famed jazz writer/critic, Leonard Feather and his wife when they came in. They looked around but couldn't find a place to sit. I got his attention and pointed to a couple of empty seats behind me close to where the tape recorder was set up, and they decided to come over and take them. As I set the reels on the machine, Leonard leaned over and introduced himself and his wife, Jane, and I in turn, introduced myself to them. I checked the reels to make sure everything was cool, and leaned forward to tell Chet.

Over the din, I was able to hear Leonard Feather talking to some other couple seated next to him. He was talking to them about Chet's injuries and how he and his wife had come to see if Chet would in fact really be able to play, or just be able to sing. They didn't want to miss it for the world.

I wasn't sure if Chet had heard Leonard Feather talking or

not, but at that precise moment, he turned around, looked over his left shoulder and nodded, then turned back around and spoke to Frank Strazzeri. "Let's do, *Blue n' Boogie*," he said, and as soon as he'd spoken, a silence filled the air. Chet turned and looked over his right shoulder and counted off the blues tune in a medium up tempo and we began to play the head, which, in jazz terms, is the actual melody played before and after the soloing choruses. Frank Strazzeri didn't play piano, but instead, played baritone horn in unison with Chet on the head, then took the first couple of choruses. Frank sounded real good, and after his solo, was followed by Chet, who was nothing short of magnificent.

Chet's phrasing was spectacular and swinging. It blew me away. Thank God I had the sense to record the night. After Chet's solo, Frank De La Rosa took a beautiful bass solo using his bow, then we did choruses and Frank joined Chet and they took the tune out. Leonard Feather leaned over to me and said how totally surprised and happy he was that Chet was actually playing again. I believe Leonard probably felt like everybody else had, that they would never get the chance to hear this great trumpet master again. Leonard was really impressed, and the look on his face said it all. He was genuinely thrilled to have been present at this historic comeback performance event.

"Chet had to come through the fires of hell to make it back this far, Leonard. And I'm proud to say, I was with him along the way." Leonard shook his head in disbelief and told me that he couldn't begin to imagine what it must have taken for Chet to play again. He told me how truly glad he was to see Chet back and how much he and his wife had always enjoyed the way Chet played their favorite song, *If You Could See Me Now*, a Tadd Dameron composition. He asked if Chet would play it for them. I told him I'd ask, but I couldn't promise anything. But I knew full well it was one of Chet's personal all-time favorite tunes, because of the history behind it.

Chet, in many of our conversations, often talked about some of the greats he'd played with. He told me how he and Tadd had known each other during the late 50s and early 60s. Their friendship had blossomed when they'd gone through a drug rehabilitation program together in Lexington, Kentucky. Later, after he returned from Europe, he and Tadd had shared Billie Holiday's old New York apartment in the West 70's. This composition of Tadd's had a deep personal significance for Chet because he'd been with him in the apartment when Tadd had taken his last breath.

I didn't mention anything to Chet about Leonard's request at that time. Chet had once mentioned to me about how he didn't really care for Leonard, and felt the feeling was probably mutual. The reason behind their apparent dislike for one another, according to Chet, had to do with the fact that Leonard Feather had this column in a jazz magazine called "The Blindfold Test." It centered on how good a jazz musician's ears were in relation to identifying a fellow musician's playing while being blindfolded. The way the test was conducted, according to what Chet told me, was that Leonard would invite a musician into a room, and place a blindfold over the musician's eyes. Then a record would be played and the blindfolded musician would then have to identify who it was that he or she were listening to.

Chet told me that he had been asked by Leonard to take the test. Chet told him straight out that he didn't have time to play 'those little kid's games,' and ever since that time Leonard Feather had never given Chet a decent review. But I figured, to hell with it, that was a different time and Chet sure as hell didn't need any bad reviews at this keenly important time in his new beginning. So I leaned forward and told Chet what Leonard had requested.

Chet turned around, looked over his shoulder and briefly acknowledged Leonard and his wife, then turned, looked at me and cupped his right hand and whispered, "Watch my hand." He then leaned his body to his right and lowered his right hand down as close as he could get it to the floor, and commenced to open and close his hand in a slow continual movement, signifying that this was how fast he wanted the time to fall on the downbeat of my Hi Hat. I told him I understood, and he turned to Frank Strazzeri and said, *If You Could See Me Now* and counted off the time.

One... Two... Three... and he began to play, and oh my God above, the tone and the notes he chose were nothing short of absolute lyrical perfection. It was unbelievable! He played it with so much depth of feeling… so haunting and poignantly beautiful that the entire audience was mesmerized in the moment. In his playing, he was actually exposing his very soul, baring it to the listeners, not only for them to hear in their hearts, but also for them to see. With every individual note he played, he was proving the medical experts, doctors, neurologists, doubters, backbiters and fair-weather friends all wrong. Chet Baker was back and I could hardly believe my good fortune to be right there with him!

He ended the tune and received a wonderful ovation. When the applause died down, he announced the rhythm section to the audience. "Thank you on behalf of Frank Strazzeri on piano, Frank De La Rosa on bass, Art Frank on drums, and myself. We'll be back in a few minutes with more music, so please stick around." There was more applause as the four of us left the stand. I thanked Chet for teaching me how to play with dynamic restraint and to be able to play in a whisper and still swing. He smiled and said something about me that I shall never forget.

He said he wouldn't be able to teach me a single thing if I didn't already have it in my heart and soul to begin with. "You're a total ear player like I am, Art, and that's what makes the difference in your playing, just like it does in mine." Coming from Chet that was to me quite a compliment. I really didn't know what to say, so I said nothing.

We went outside for a smoke, and were joined seconds later by television star Dennis Cole and his date, Carole Curb. Dennis introduced himself and Carole to me, then quickly to Chet, telling him how truly happy he was to meet him and how much he loved his playing, and that he'd also been a long time, major fan.

Chet smiled and told Dennis that he was also a fan of his. When he said that, Dennis' face came alive with excitement and disbelief. Chet told him that he had seen him on his television series, *Felony Squad*, and really liked his acting. Dennis looked surprised to learn that Chet liked his acting, and doubly surprised to hear that Chet had also called himself a fan of his as well.

The four of us stood outside talking about Chet and his comeback and future plans until Frank Strazzeri came outside and told Chet that the owner was looking for us to begin the third set. Chet waved to Frank and told him we'd be in shortly. Dennis and Carole excused themselves and went back inside while we remained behind and finished our cigarettes. I was thinking to myself what a wonderful evening we'd been having, when all of a sudden, Chet's nose started to run again. I had a handkerchief in my back pocket and quickly gave it to him, and asked if he thought he'd be able to able to make it through the third set.

"Let's go in. I'll make it through, man," he said, and he sure as hell did, too. The night ended on an upbeat with the club owner coming over and asking Chet if he'd be free to play a few more nights, beginning Tuesday of the coming week. Chet needed the work, and the bread, and told the owner we'd be there.

Chapter 24
Leonard Feather's Review

TRUMPETER CHET BAKER AT THE MELODY ROOM

> Trumpeter Chet Baker's booking at the Melody Room not only marks a return to jazz for that erratically directed Sunset Strip spot, but also Baker's first extended Hollywood job in years...
>
> What went on at the Melody Room was just basic blowing-theme, ad lib choruses, theme. At times Baker seemed to falter or lose the thread of a melodic line, but for the most part, he was as sensitively self-expressive as ever.
>
> **Leonard Feather**
> (Los Angeles Times, Feb.11, 1969)

For the record, let me just say, Chet didn't falter, nor did he ever '*lose the thread of a melodic line!*' That would have been next to impossible for Chet, because he knew the melodies of every tune he ever played inside out. He was without question, the absolute master of the melodic and lyrical line! I believe Leonard didn't take into consideration how much Chet had to go through just to be able to play again, along with the fact that his approach had changed. He was more introspective, brooding and halting. He'd play a melodic line for a few bars, then suddenly stop purposely for a bar, or two or three, allowing the rhythm section to churn and then pick up the melodic thread again, which signaled a new stage in his playing and to my ears was beautiful! This new style was being developed with each note Chet played, and I believe this is what Leonard Feather heard, and mistook it as Chet faltering or losing the melodic thread.

Chet played, on average, a half octave lower than the average trumpet player did. And he had this absolute penchant for understatement and unhurriedness that was so compelling. He always played a little on the dark side of the note, and would like to hold on to the note he was playing until he found one of equal value and meaning before moving on to the next. His phrasing was also far different than any other player, in that he played in what he called, a sort of a 'percussive Stop and Go' mode - meaning that he'd begin a phrase, stop it and allow the time to go by for a couple bars, then pick up the phrase line again and continue on. He played in what could also be called a 'broken rhythm' style in that he would play a series of short, just behind the beat phrases, then long tones, followed by a rapid fire sequence of perfectly placed eight notes strung together in such a way that the effect was like a beautifully strung necklace of sheer melodic, lyrical beauty.

His sound was pensive, thought-filled and melancholic, always with a touch of sadness, up-tempo or dirge-like balladry. The way he played, his particular choice of notes, and his special way of shaping and articulating them, put him in a class all by himself. His playing seemed effortless, but I can assure you it wasn't. He worked for every note he played.

He once told me this analogy about how he set up his improvisational ideas. He said it was like walking into a completely strange room he'd never been in before. He'd take a step in, then a step back, then a step forward, another step forward and another, familiarizing himself with the area. He'd see a set of stairs and go up slowly, reaching the landing, walk around a little then come back down over the stairs fast. And sometimes, on some tunes, he would use the special tone and sound that separated him from all other trumpet players - a soft, velvet, wispy sound where you could hear the flow of air going through the horn followed by the sound itself.

Really quite unique! Chet had this 'just behind the beat' kind of phrasing that would cause the listener to think that he wasn't going to quite make the next note or phrase. But this wasn't because he had any kind of problem with the command of his instrument, he assuredly didn't. Chet had absolute perfect control, and knew precisely what he was going to do a millisecond before he did it. And somehow, through the grace of God, I seemed to know it too.

Chapter 25
Herb Alpert at A&M Studios

The morning, following Sunday night's gig, Chet showed up at my house in the brown Caddy his mother had bought for him. When he came in I showed him the newspaper article by Leonard Feather. He scanned it quickly, and with a look of disgust, laid it on the table without saying a word. I asked him what had brought him to Culver City so early in the day, and he said he was having trouble with his car, and wanted me to take a ride with him to see if I could help him figure out what might be wrong with it.

We drove down to Venice Beach and back. During the drive I could feel the front end was a little shaky and told him he'd probably need to have new shocks installed, and have the front end aligned. He had a mechanic out in the San Fernando Valley, so I followed him in my car so he could drop his off and I'd give him a ride back home to Redondo Beach.

There was a Winchell's Donut Shop next door to the mechanic shop in Encino, so we, of course, indulged in a coffee and jelly donut. After a brief conversation with the mechanic, we got into my car and jumped back onto the freeway. As we were nearing the Hollywood exits, Chet suddenly sat up in his seat.

"I just remembered. I'm supposed to be meeting with Herb at A&M today. You want to make it over there with me?" he asked. I told him I would get off the freeway in Hollywood.

A&M Studios was located on the corner of Sunset and La Brea. Chet wanted me to accompany him in to see Herb but I felt it would probably be better for the two of them to talk privately because in that way, both men would be able to speak without reserve. I heard a Brazilian group playing in one of the studios and pointed it out to Chet.

"Those cats in there sound pretty groovy. Think I'll go in and check 'em out. I'll wait for you in there." He nodded and I went into the studio and took a seat against the rear wall and watched and listened to the Brazilian group running through some rehearsals on the stage. These guys were great! The tunes were very melodic, rhythmic, yet with a hint of sadness. Man, I couldn't keep from tapping my feet and snapping my fingers. I must have listened to them for at least 45 minutes, until they had finished their rehearsal and came down off the stand. As one of them approached the door, I spoke up and told him how really great I thought they were.

I introduced myself to him, telling him that I was there waiting while Chet was at the studio visiting with Herb. He got real excited when I mentioned that Chet was close by and said he'd really like to get the chance to meet him. He was a member of Sergio Mendes' band, and that Sergio himself was a great fan of Chet's as well. He also told me that he felt Sergio would also like to meet Chet.

I'd heard the name Sergio Mendes mentioned before, but at that particular point in time, he was nowhere as famous as he was soon to become. I promised to introduce him to Chet as soon as he came in to get me, but he didn't return for nearly another hour, so the man and Sergio reluctantly had to leave without getting the chance to meet him. A short time after they left, the door opened and there stood Chet with this big happy smile on his face.

"How'd it go with Herb?"

"Well, it was great. Herb was very cool. He asked about Carol and the kids, and how I was doing. He could have just sat back behind his desk and looked down on me, but he didn't. He was cool, and told me how really glad he was that I was playing again, and how he had always respected who I was and the way I played…" He stopped, and didn't say another thing for almost a minute. When he did speak, it wasn't about music or the like but about Herb's generosity of heart toward his fellow man. And to Chet, that meant more to him than a million unfelt spoken words.

I was so happy that Herb had given him the respect he so deserved. Chet really needed someone of Herb's stature to help lift his spirits, especially at such a crucial time in his life. "He even laid some bread on me, too, man." Chet said happily.

"God bless him! And from now on I'm a fan of Herb Alpert." I said, and we both laughed happily.

"Well, it's like I said… Herb is the only record producer willing to give me a helping hand. He's one of a kind, Art. One of a kind…" he said with a quiet appreciation. I absolutely agreed.

On the drive home, we talked about Herb quite a lot. That was another special thing about Chet. If he liked a person, he'd speak of him often. But if he didn't, he wouldn't even mention the person's name, except for one in particular – Richard Carpenter, his one-time manager. But that's another story. Chet closed his eyes and settled back into the seat, and for the first time in a long time, he looked relaxed and at peace.

Chapter 26
Stop and Go

The following day it was raining again, so I decided it would be a good idea to eat an earlier supper than usual so I could pick Chet up and make it to The Melody Room with a little time to spare. This way Chet could greet his fans before we went up on the stand.

By the time we arrived at the club it was going on 8:30 p.m. There weren't a lot of people in the club at that time which made me think perhaps it was going to be a slow night. But by the time ten o'clock rolled around there were a good 45 to 50 people... not bad for a Tuesday night.

Chet always sat whenever he had the chance. Mostly because he suffered from a lot of lower back pain brought on by all the years of traveling from city to city and country to country. Anyway, on this one particular night, Chet was seated on the stand, eyes closed, playing beautifully, when from out of nowhere, Tony, the owner of the Melody Room came boldly up and confronted him. Chet was surprised to see the man looking down at him with an angry look on his face. Chet, trying to be a gentleman, asked him what he was doing on the stand.

"I came up to see how bad you were... and you're very bad tonight! If you're gonna play then, stand up for God's sake!" he said angrily. Then he turned and walked down off the stand and back behind the bar. I was really pissed at that little bastard for addressing Chet in that manner and tone, but took it from the source from whence it came. The owner didn't know a thing about jazz. Chet fluffed it off, remained seated and played the tune out. We took a break and joined Sally and Honey Bruce who were seated along the front section of the horseshoe bar, and spent a few minutes with them. Shortly after that the door opened and in walked one of the pushers who had been hanging around the club trying to entice Chet into buying junk. I nudged Chet and he turned and gave the guy a quick glance, then looked back to me.

"If that clown tries to sell you anything, I'll kick his lousy ass all over Sunset Boulevard! And I mean it!" I wanted Chet to know I was only looking out for his behalf. He gave me a smile and got up off the stool and walked outside with the man while I waited nervously with Sally and Honey. I didn't have very long to wait before Chet calmly walked back in. I tried to read his facial expression, but couldn't. I had no real idea whether he had bought anything from the pusher or not, and he wasn't saying one way or the other. We went back up onto the stand. Before we played, Chet came over and let me know he'd told the pusher he wasn't interested and the guy split. I was really glad he told me, and thankful he sent the guy away. We finished the last two sets and called it a night.

It was still raining when we got outside. I was real tired and couldn't wait to get home and get into bed. There was nothing quite as cozy as being in a warm bed on a cold night listening to the rain hitting the ground hard just outside your window. That cozy thought quickly vanished when Chet reminded me of my promise to drive him over to the Valley after the gig to pick up his car. The mechanic was a friend of his and had agreed to meet him there after hours. I really didn't want to drive over there in this hard falling rain, but, this was Chet and I had given my word.

There wasn't a lot of traffic on the surface streets at 1:30 in the a.m., which at least made driving a lot easier. Once I got onto the freeway, the subject of Sally Bruce, Lenny's mother came up, along with Lenny's use of heroin and his untimely death. I mentioned again how much Sally really liked Chet, and how much he reminded her of Lenny. She worried that Chet would wind up the same way. I glanced at Chet and told him how bad I felt that Lenny had died so young, but he didn't respond.

I became worried about his silence and decided to be more direct.

"You're not taking that shit any more are you, Chet?" He didn't answer. "I wouldn't ever want to see anything like what happened to Lenny Bruce happen to you, man. You've got a lot more playing to do, so you gotta take care of yourself, you know what I'm saying?" He still didn't respond. I figured that while I had him in the car, he had no choice but to listen to what I was saying whether he liked it or not. It was a calculated risk. He could tell me to mind my own business, go to hell, or he could listen.

"Listen man, I love you, and so does your family. If I didn't care I wouldn't be saying a fucking thing."

He turned and looked at me painfully. "I know that, Art, but… I'm really not hurting anyone you know?"

"You may not be hurting anyone, but you're taking away from us. Think about it, man. You're taking away from yourself, Carol, the kids, your mother, me and Earla… and your fans."

"Well, I'm sorry about that, man… but I don't really see where I'm hurting or taking away from anyone, you know?" He meant what he said. He genuinely felt he wasn't hurting anyone. And in his own way, telling me to mind my own business.

"I don't really know what it's like, but I can't see how taking any of that shit could be any good for anybody."

"Well, hopefully you'll never find out, Art," he replied quietly. I could see he didn't want to talk about it, so I clammed up until we got off the freeway.

I spotted the Winchell's next to the garage, and asked if he could go for a coffee and doughnut. He liked the idea, so I pulled over and went inside. They didn't have any jelly doughnuts so we settled for chocolate éclairs. We finished up with a cigarette and coffee. Chet asked me to stick around until he made sure his car was ready to go. He went next door and disappeared inside the dimly lit garage. He was gone for at least 20 minutes and when he came back he appeared wide-awake and together.

"Everything cool with the shocks, Chet?"

"Yeah, he put in new front shocks, upper ball joint bearings and aligned the front end."

"You need any bread to help cover the bill?"

"It's already covered, man,' he answered with a smile. "The guy plays a little trumpet but couldn't make a living with it so he opened up his own little garage to make a buck. He's a fan of mine, so we worked out a deal. He just charged for the cost of the parts. I told him I'd give him a couple of lessons and autograph a few of his albums, and he was cool with that."

Chet took care of the check and we went outside into the rain. I told him I'd follow him as far as Culver City to make sure the car was cool. He smiled and then ran over to his car, turned on the ignition, the lights, backed out onto the street and literally zoomed off toward the freeway, leaving a trail of rain and road dirt in his wake. I got right in behind him and followed him onto the freeway.

Man, I had no idea how dangerously fast Chet liked to drive until I followed him on the rain-slicked freeway. He must have been doing between 90 and 100 miles an hour because the red color from his tail lights soon became nothing but a blur due to both the speed and the effect of the wind-ripped rain being lifted up by his rear tires. He must have been a good quarter of a mile ahead and still pulling away.

I was scared as hell he was going to crash and kept on praying. He rounded a long curve and disappeared out of view. When I finally arrived at the same curve and looked up ahead, I saw absolutely nothing. His car had completely vanished. I slowed down to about 55 and stayed close to the extreme right side of the road looking into the crevices and alongside the mountains to see if maybe his car might have hydroplaned and crashed, but I didn't see any sign of the car.

I had never seen anyone drive quite like that before. I thought maybe he was challenging death like the late James Dean used to do, or maybe he was just trying to impress me, like he had absolutely no fear of anyone or anything. Maybe. But I'd seen the apprehension he displayed just a few days ago on the opening night of his comeback, so I knew he could feel fear. A paradox? I didn't know for sure. But whatever it was, I was still very concerned and decided to drive past the Culver City off ramp and continue on looking for any signs of an accident. Thank God there were none. I figured he would, in all probability make it home safely. After about fifteen miles, I turned around and drove home and went to bed. It was still raining hard outside, and as I got under the covers, I offered up a prayer for Chet's safety.

The following night I was at the bar in The Melody Room

having a beer when Frank Strazzeri walked over to say hello. I was still nervous about Chet, wondering if he had made it home safely or not. Just as I was about to ask Frank if he had heard from Chet, he walked in and came right over to where I was and gave me a hug. "Man, am I ever glad to see you!!" I told him. "You scared the fucking shit out of me last night man! I thought for sure you'd crack up somewhere along the way, man"

Chet opened his eyes wide and chuckled lightly. "Why... I was only doing a hundred and ten."

I was flabbergasted to say the least, and would come to learn that the sheer anticipation and excitement of driving a car fast always exhilarated Chet, no matter what the weather conditions or the condition of the roads. He just seemed to become completely alert and alive as soon as he sat behind the wheel of a car.

It was a bit slow in the club, but a few more people were starting to come in, and that really pleased the owner. He came over to Chet and told him to get the musicians on the stand and start playing right away because he didn't want to lose any business. His attitude pissed me off, but I remained cool. Hell, it was a Wednesday night and there weren't as many people in the club as there had been on the weekend nights. Chet was clearly pissed off too, and I thought for sure he was going to grab Tony and kick his ass, but quickly thought the better of it. Chet started up on the stand and we followed.

Chet opened with the blues tune *Blue 'n' Boogie*. His playing was unbelievable and ineffably swinging. We played another tune, *Look for the Silver Lining* and Chet sang and played it beautifully.

The rest of the night was uneventful, except when one of the pushers I'd seen coming into the club before came in and stood near the bar. Pushers reminded me of hungry vultures waiting for Chet to weaken so he'd want to buy their shit. They didn't give a damn about how hard he was fighting to control his body's cravings. All they cared about was getting him back on their list of users so they'd be able to follow him around to whatever club he might be playing and sell him their garbage. But God bless Chet because he didn't weaken, he just continued to take his pain pills and fight his body's urges, and man, that made me so happy and proud of him.

We ended the tune and played another before taking a break. As soon as we came down off the stand, the pusher immediately made his way over to Chet like a spider moving down its web to encircle a captured fly. I made sure I was right there beside Chet when he confronted him. And without blinking, gave him a cold menacing stare and told the guy to get lost or I'd put him through a fucking wall. I continued to stare at him coldly for a few seconds, waiting to see if he wanted to challenge me, but he didn't, and instead, turned and left the club. I confided to Chet that I'd actually been a little nervous there for a couple minutes. The guy could have been packing a rod, and could've blown my guts all over the fucking place.

Chet laughed and said he'd told the pushers not to fuck with me because I was real good with my hands and loved to kick the shit out of people just for the fun of it. I laughed.

"No wonder they split so quickly," I said. We both had a laugh over that one.

For the record, I can honestly say that I never saw Chet buying any kind of drugs from any of the pushers that frequented the club or those who hung around outside. For one thing, he couldn't have even if he'd wanted to because we weren't making enough bread from Tony to begin with. We were being paid scale, and that was it.

While we were out having a smoke, the club door opened and several of Chet's fans came outside, holding some of his albums, asking for his autograph, which he graciously did. They thanked him and went back into the club just as Frankie Avalon was coming out of the club. He walked up to us and introduced himself. He asked if he could sit in and play trumpet with the group in the next set. Chet told him he could, and that he'd call him up. Frankie thanked him, shook his hand and went back into the club.

"Think he can play?" I asked Chet.

He shrugged his shoulders. "Well, I'm sure he can play some tune," he said and then headed back inside to finish the last set.

The four of us went up onto the stand and Chet introduced Frankie Avalon, and invited him to come up and play a tune, which he happily did. Frankie called for a standard and played quite well. He wasn't a bop player by any stretch of the imagination, but he did play pretty damn well. When the tune ended he received a nice round of applause as he left the bandstand.

Chet called an up-tempo tune, *Here I'll Stay*, to let the rhythm section stretch out a bit. After we ended that tune, a woman in the audience requested a popular ballad, *When I Fall in Love*. Chet played it beautifully. Whenever he played a ballad, there was always a personal sadness and poignancy connected to it, as though he were playing it just for you. His solos were like romantic sonnets. He once told me that ballads were the real test of player – because there's nowhere to hide.

We played a few more tunes then ended the night. We were about to leave when the club owner came over and asked Chet if he wanted to do a few more nights at the club. Chet looked at me and I quickly nodded in the affirmative. He told Tony we would. That made the night special for me because it meant I'd have the chance to perform with Chet for at least a few more nights. Man, was I ever happy!

Chapter 27
A Few More Nights

We were now booked at The Melody Room through Sunday. Everything was going along beautifully until Thursday morning rolled around. I received a phone call from Frank De La Rosa, the great bassist who'd been playing with us, informing me he couldn't make the gig that night because he had to go back on the road with Ella Fitzgerald's group. This meant I'd have to find somebody else to take his place as soon as possible. Needless to say, I was very concerned because I knew how difficult it was going to be to find a bassist anywhere close to Frank's caliber to play behind Chet; and if I did, would he be available?

I sat down and called nine or ten different bass players in succession but not one of them was free that night. I made more calls and received the same answer. Angry and frustrated, I slammed the receiver forcefully into the base cradle nearly cracking the phone in half. Earla had heard me from the other room and came out to see what I was getting so upset about. I explained my plight and she understood completely.

The two of us sat there for nearly an hour trying to think of various bass players I could call, but to no avail. Then I remembered a car salesman acquaintance whose friend played bass, albeit, rock, so I gave him a call and asked him to find out if the guy would be available to play, and if he felt his friend would be good enough to play with the likes of Chet Baker. He told me he'd contact the bass player and have him give me a call and we could talk things over. I thanked him and waited for the call.

Later that afternoon a very excited young man called and introduced himself as Bob Johnston, or something like that, and told me he was a bass player, and that although he'd be very nervous about playing with a musician of Chet's stature, he'd be willing to give it his all and try. I asked if he played upright and he said no, that he only played electric. I told him that Chet wouldn't like the idea one bit, but I felt sure it would be all right. I told him to be at the Melody Room around 8 p.m. to meet our pianist, Frank Strazzeri, to go over the tunes.

I told Earla all about it, and how concerned I was about hiring an electric bass player without Chet's knowledge or approval.

"What if the guy can't play more than three changes? What if he can't hold the time? What if he can't improvise?" I was very nervous, because when Chet was on the stand, he was a whole different man... an absolute perfectionist. Before I met him, I'd read in jazz magazines about Chet's reputation in these types of situations. I knew if this cat couldn't cut it, Chet would kick his ass off the stand, then ream my ass for getting someone before knowing whether they could play or not.

"You're doing the best you can under the circumstances. I'm sure Chet will appreciate that," Earla said. I hoped she was right but wouldn't count on it. Even though Chet was only into the second week of his comeback, he didn't tolerate mistakes when he was playing.

Earla and I arrived at the Melody Room around 8:15 p.m. and chatted with Frank Strazzeri who had just arrived a few minutes earlier. I hipped him to the new bass player, informing him that he played electric and that I really didn't know how good he was, or how Chet was going to react. I no more than completed my sentence when the door opened and in walked a young man around 25 years old, carrying long black guitar case.

He strolled up to the bar where we were standing and introduced himself to each of us, his excitement very clear. Frank invited him up to the stand to go over the lead sheets and to run through a few tunes while Earla nursed a glass of red wine and I, a cold bottle of beer. The kid removed his bass and plugged it into an outlet and tuned up against the notes Frank gave him.

I thought he had a nice full sound, and was also able to hold down the time and tempo. It was nearing 9 p.m., which meant we'd be going up to play soon so Frank put the young bass player through a few more changes and he seemed to be handling it well until the door opened and Chet walked in. The young man became even more excited by his presence.

Chet looked up to the stand curiously as he made his way over to Earla and me.

"Who's that cat, man?" Chet asked evenly.

I explained what had happened with Frank De La Rosa, and how I had called every bass player in L.A. but they all had gigs. The guy on the stand was the only one available. I told Chet I hadn't heard him but the guy assured me he could play.

Chet watched and listened to him curiously, turned to me. "You know I can't stand any electronic shit, man," he said.

"I know that, man, but what could I do? I had to get somebody. You think he'll be OK for the night?"

He shrugged. "We'll have to wait and see, man," he replied.

Chet took his seat in the chair directly in front of my drums. I sat down on my stool and introduced Chet to Bob who held out his hand nervously, and the two briefly shook hands. Frank leaned over and asked Chet what he wanted to open with. He thought about it for a minute or so.

"Let's do *Another You.*" He counted off the time in a medium tempo and sang the first chorus and played on the second with Frank taking a couple of choruses, then giving the bassist a chance to take a chorus or two. As soon as he began, it became painfully clear that the guy was not a strong jazz bassist because he just didn't know how to improvise all that melodically, and instead, just played a kind of a steady thumping sound. I thought for sure Chet was going to bounce him off the stand right then and there, but for some reason, he did not. Chet sang the last chorus and ended the tune. He turned his head around over his right shoulder and speared me an icy glare, then turned back towards Frank and called out a second tune. Before we could play it, some lady in the audience requested *My Funny Valentine*. So he called that one instead.

This was Chet's signature tune and I wasn't sure the bassist had ever played it the way we were going to play it. Chet kicked off very slowly and sure enough, when Chet started to sing, the guy really wasn't familiar with the tune, so Frank had to call out each chord change to him, which totally unnerved Chet, who somehow managed to keep his cool until the end of the tune. Chet was visibly upset and was about to jump all over the guy's ass but the audience response was so appreciative, he decided to let it slide. He smiled briefly and called out, *On Green Dolphin Street*.

"Oh no," I thought to myself. "There was no way this cat was going to be able to cut it." And I was so right. All during the tune, Frank had to continually call out the changes to him and this really got to Chet.

He stopped playing abruptly and called out, exasperated. "I can't take... I can't take it!" Chet said disgustedly. "There's no...TONE! There's just a steady boom, boom, boom." He looked over his shoulder at me and he was pissed. But didn't really say anything to hurt the guy's feelings.

"I thought he'd be cool for the night, Chet," I said apologetically. "He was the only one available, man."

That obviously wasn't good enough for Chet. "Well, you should have known better than to hire somebody who can't play standards, man, you know?"

"I did the best I could, man! What the hell do you want me to do about it now?" I replied.

"Well, you can take your fuckin' brushes and go paint a house, man," he fired back.

"Alright man, fuck it!"

Now Chet was forever telling me how much he loved the way I played brushes behind him. I also knew him well enough to know that he really didn't mean for it to come out the way it did. He was pissed because I'd hired a bass player who was really not seasoned enough to lay down the harmonic lines he needed to hear. However, even knowing that, I was pretty angry myself.

I got up, grabbed my sticks and brushes, walked down off the stand and stood by the bar. The poor young bass player packed up his bass and walk out of the club. Earla came right over and asked what had happened. I told her and she advised me to just be cool, that maybe Chet would come down and apologize to me after the set.

Chet went on to finish the set minus drums and bass, and when he came down off the stand, he shot me a look, but didn't say a word.

"Let's get outta here," I said to Earla. We left the club and drove home, talking about what I was going to do the following night. Was I going to go back to the club to see if Chet would apologize? And if not, I'd just pack my drums and let the chips fall where they may.

The following night, which was a Friday, I went up to The Melody Room and got there around 8:45 p.m. I sat at the bar talking with Sally and Honey Bruce, who both seemed to be there every night. As we sat there talking, Chet came over and gave Sally a warm hug and kiss on the cheek, greeted Honey and sat down right beside me. We just looked at one another.

"Did you bring your sticks and brushes with you, man?" he asked with that Chet Baker smile. I told him I had and took them out of my pants pocket and held them up for him to see.

"I know it was only for a couple of sets, but I missed you behind me, man," he said, and wrapped his arms around me. And that was the end of it.

"You'll like who I've got on bass for the next two nights."

We went up onto the stage and who's going over tunes with Frank Strazzeri but the great Jimmy Gannon. We were both surprised to see each other, shook hands and within minutes, the four of us were swinging. We finished that night, and had a near full house for the following Saturday and Sunday nights. So both Chet and I figured that Tony, the club owner, would be asking Chet to do another week because business had been so good, but he didn't. Instead, he informed us that he had hired a rock group for the following week.

After the last night of the gig, Chet and I were hungry so we decided to go to Denny's on Sunset. Chet was a fan of silver dollar size with his eggs over easy rather than scrambled and after we dusted off the pancakes and ordered more coffee, we lit up cigarettes and talked about the next gig and where it might be.

We were both a little down, especially Chet because he really needed the work, the bread and the exposure. I assured him everything was going to be all right, and reminded him that I'd be making phone calls to all the club owners and managers around L.A. during the following week. Privately, I didn't hold out much hope of getting him any gigs. I hadn't seen a club owner come to the club to check him out, which I felt was strange considering he'd been doing great business for Tony while we were there. I never did see Hal Cohn again after our last night at the

Melody Room. I've often wondered what happened to him.

"I went to see Shelly at his club a couple nights ago and had a long talk with him," I told Chet. "I let him know you were playing pretty good now and how great it would be if he were to give you a week at The Manne Hole. He said he was sorry but his club was booked solid for a year."

When Chet heard that, he was very dubious and made a face. "That's not the reason," he said. "No club owner books a year in advance. He's afraid to hire me. He thinks I'm still on the shit and won't show up for the gig. And if I did, would I be straight or nodding out?"

"I don't know what his real reason was, but as far as I'm concerned, Shelly is wrong for not giving you a week at his club. You'd have packed that place every friggin' night."

Chet shook his head slowly and looked out the window obviously pained. I could feel his hurt almost as much as he did. I couldn't figure out why club owners and musicians, in general, continued to make excuses and turn their backs on Chet. It didn't make any sense when you consider that Chet had previously hired a lot of the same musicians who now wanted little or nothing to do with him. Not one of them had the balls to step up to help him in his time of need.

"Well... the world's a cold fucking place, man. The only time people want you around is when you can do something for them. Otherwise you're no fucking good to them," he said with mild disgust.

I racked my brain trying to think of someone who might be willing to help Chet.

"What about Art Pepper, Chet? You think he'd help you?"

"No... no, I really don't think Art would care to help me either," he said discouraged. I asked why, but he wasn't anxious to talk about it, so I let the idea go. "He couldn't help me anyway because he's in Synanon." I asked what he meant, and was told Synanon was a drug rehabilitation center in Santa Monica Beach where most professional people go to get themselves straightened out.

"Oh! Well, I wish Art the best. I always dug his playing. He's one of my all-time favorite alto players. Bird... Stitt... Pepper, those three... It doesn't get any better than that. Art's playing reminds me a lot of you because he lays everything he's got in his heart right out there for the world to hear."

"Yeah... Art's a great player. I've always dug his phrasing, too." A sudden thought came into his mind and he smiled. "You know, I've got three different cats named Art in my address book. Art Pepper. The one I used to get my shit from, and yours. So, I added an extra 't' to your name so I wouldn't wind up calling the wrong Art, you know?" he said. Who else but Chet would have come up with an idea like that?

"That's a pretty hip thing, man," I said, and took out a pen and wrote it out on a napkin. "Man, it looks weird, but I'm going to keep it. I'll probably be the only other guy named Art to spell his name with two t's."

Chet was about to say something else when something just outside the restaurant window grabbed his attention and he gestured for me to look. An old bum was going through a trash can. "Look at that poor cat. It's nearly three o'clock in the morning, we're on Sunset Boulevard in Hollywood, and that poor cat's got half his body in the trash barrel trying to find himself a little something to eat. Do you think anyone gives a shit about him, man?"

"It sure as hell doesn't look like anybody does."

"I don't think anyone would care if the guy lived or died, They probably wouldn't even notice, you know?" With that, he got up out of the booth, went outside, walked up to the old man, reached into his pocket and gave the guy whatever he had. Without saying a word, he turned around and came back into the restaurant and sat down again.

Here was a man whose one-time friends had so uncaringly turned their backs on him – a man who the music world no longer cared about, who took his last few dollars and gave it to an old, poor stranger. I'll never forget that.

Chapter 28
Fathers and Sons

We stayed a while longer at the Denny's, smoking and drinking more coffee. The sight of the poor man digging for food, and Chet's immediate selfless act, triggered his memory to a more spiritual time in his childhood. And although Chet had made the claim of not believing in the Biblical God, he did believe in a supreme being, which was in essence the same. Through my daily mentioning of God and Jesus, I really felt Chet was coming to believe. He told me that his dad used to drink a lot, but on rare occasions, would read the Bible.

I told him that my father wasn't perfect but that he read the Bible every day. My dad once told me that if a person started off poor and somehow struck it rich, and forgot where he or she had come from, then a person such as this would find little difficulty in stuffing up their ears against the cries of a starving child or the homeless.

Chet agreed with my father's wisdom, and told me that even though his father was also far from perfect, he had likewise taught him a couple of valuable lessons from the Bible as well, such as how giving to the less fortunate was always the right thing to do.

His father's teaching had clearly sunk in. I had been witness on several occasions of the compassion, sensitivity and sympathy he held for the poor and less fortunate. And, as I was about to learn, this also extended to family.

A soft smile had spread over Chet's face as we sat there in that Denny's, looking out onto Sunset Boulevard. The more he reflected on whatever it was he was thinking about, the wider the smile became. I was very curious and asked what was going on.

He told me about this one night when he was playing at some

club with his own quartet. This was after he had split with the Gerry Mulligan Quartet. During one of their breaks, Chet had gone to the bathroom, and unbeknownst to him, had walked right past his father seated at the bar. If he hadn't gone over to see the bartender about something on his way back, he probably wouldn't have noticed his dad sitting there.

As Chet told it, he went over to his dad, asked how he was and what he was doing there, but his father didn't answer him. Chet said he asked again, and this time his dad told him there was nothing wrong, that he was just having a drink and listening to the music. But Chet knew better. He could see something was hurting him. He said he put his arm around his father's shoulder, hugged him and said he wanted to help.

He said his father looked at him with tears glistening in his eyes and painfully related to him how he had come out to California hoping to make something of himself in the music field, and instead, got stuck in an airplane factory doing manual labor. He told me how sad his father was, and how much he missed playing for people, and how he felt the people had really liked his playing in Oklahoma. He told Chet that it seemed nobody gave a damn about his banjo and guitar playing anymore. Chet said his father rubbed his eyes with his coat sleeve and turned away so Chet wouldn't see the tears.

He didn't know what to do when he saw the tears in his father's eyes. He said the two of them just stood there not knowing what to say or what to do. They loved each other, but neither knew quite how to express it one to the other.

"So what'd you do?" I asked

"I told him I felt like I owed a lot of my success to him because if he hadn't bought me that trumpet I probably would have wound up pumping gas or something else."

He said when his dad heard that, he started to both cry and laugh at the same time. He said he also asked if he and his mother wanted to spend a couple of weeks in Miami to hear him and his group play. His father told him that he couldn't because he and his mother had to work.

Chet told his father to forget about the factory and to take a couple of months off and travel with him and act as his personal manager. Chet said his father got up off the bar stool and hugged him hard, and asked him several times if he really meant what he'd said about his being his manager. Chet said he assured him he did and the two shook hands cementing the verbal contract.

I was puzzled and asked him why he wanted his father to be his manager, especially in light of the fact that he still liked to tip the bottle and all. Chet said he loved his dad and wanted to get him away from the factory for a while so the two could spend more time together. And maybe even set up an opportunity for his dad to play his banjo for a live audience.

He went on to talk about how a few days later he and his father and three other musicians, two white and one black, traveled to Florida in Chet's Jaguar. They'd spotted a family restaurant about 50 miles outside of Miami, and everyone wanted to stop to grab a bite to eat. He said when he pulled into the parking lot, his father, had been drinking a bottle of beer, and when the five of them got out of the car, the half empty bottle fell out of his dad's hand and broke into pieces on the cement. Chet said he was pissed because he didn't like the idea of his dad drinking beer, period! Let along drinking it in his car. But for the moment, he didn't say a word because he didn't want to embarrass his dad in front of the musicians. He did say that he let his father know about it later that night in their room.

They went into the family restaurant and grabbed a big booth at the end of the room. As soon as they sat down, some big tall man who was standing behind the counter looked over to them and angrily jabbed the air with a pointed finger toward the black musician. Chet asked the guy why he was pointing his finger, and the man pointed to the exit and told him gruffly that their restaurant didn't serve colored people, as they referred to them in those days. If any one of them expected to get anything to eat, the colored man would have to leave.

Chet said he was pissed and insulted and demanded to know why his friend couldn't eat with him and the others. The owner told them it was against the law, and that was that. Chet was furious and ready to toss the table settings onto the floor, but the black musician told him that it was cool. He would wait outside in the car until they finished eating, and he left the restaurant. I asked Chet if he and the others had stayed and had something to eat. His eyes opened wide and he laughed and told me he decided to beat that racist bastard at his own game. He said the owner came over to their table and asked them if they were ready to order, and Chet said he ordered five of their best steaks, four to eat there and one to go.

A few minutes went by and the owner returned to their table carrying a big platter, which he sat down on a table next to them. He placed plates of steak on the table in front of each man and set the order to go on the table to the right of Chet.

Chet said his dad put his nose directly over the steak, smelled it and looked up at the owner and told him how luscious they looked. He said the owner told him they ought to be because they were the restaurant's finest prime rib.

As soon as the owner said that, Chet told me that he and the others stood up and left the food untouched and, without saying a word, headed for the exit. The dumbfounded owner chased after them, asking which one of them was going to pay the bill for the steaks. Chet said he turned around and told the owner that he and his friends never paid the tab for food they hadn't eaten, and that was the law, too.

He told me whoever made up those segregated laws should be busted themselves. I told him I couldn't agree more.

I asked him how the gig in Miami went having his dad along as manager. He smiled and told me that he had called his group together while his dad was having a drink at the bar, and told them that later on that night they were going to surprise his father and play, *I'm An Old Cowhand* and ask him to play his banjo along with them.

He told his father to bring his banjo along with him to the club that night because he wanted him to sit in with the group. He said his dad didn't really believe him but brought it along with him just in case. During the second set, when the audience was really into his playing, he nodded to his band mates and they started to play *I'm An Old Cowhand.* He said his father, who was sitting directly in front of the bandstand, immediately recognized the tune, and quickly reached for his banjo and accompanied along with the group. Chet let his father take a solo while he stood back and watched with pride. After a few bars he said he took up his horn and he and his father brought the tune to an end much to the delight of the audience.

After that night he said his father continued to drink more and more, and by the end of the week, had run up such a large bar tab that most of the money owed to Chet was gone. On top of that, his dad even began criticizing about how Chet should be playing his trumpet. Chet told his father that he knew how to play and he'd won all the major polls, which his dad took badly, feeling that Chet was just like his mother, who never listened to what he had to say, and that Chet didn't really care about him. Exasperated, Chet told his father he did love him, but because he was either drinking or hanging with his friends, Chet was never allowed to show him. His father's feelings were hurt by that remark, so Chet cooled it and told him that he didn't want to spend time arguing.

Sitting there, all these years later, Chet inhaled deeply and breathed out a long weary sigh. He confided that he felt that success had come too fast for him to adjust to, especially in some of his personal relationships.

Another long sigh escaped his lips as he talked about his divorce from his second wife, Halema, a beautiful East Indian girl. There was another long pause before he spoke fondly of when she'd given birth to their son, Chesney Aftab, and his concerns at that time about being able to take care of the two of them due to his constantly being on the road. It was equally difficult then, as he was also dealing with the personal loss of his friends, Charlie Parker and Dick Twardzik in the same year.

Chet said he talked things over with his father and decided it would be much easier for the both of them if his dad went back home to California.

Although their professional collaboration couldn't be sustained, at least this father and son had been able, for a brief time, to share the stage and play the music they both lived for. It was a gift I'd often dreamed of sharing with my dad.

Chapter 29
Marking Time

After the gig at The Melody Room ended I felt a real let down because it meant I didn't have any idea when Chet and I would be working together again. I mean, there were a few good clubs and all, but most of the managers were new and unfamiliar to me and they tended to hire the musicians they liked and who were 'radio popular' at that time. Our chances of playing together again in L.A. were at best, slim to none.

As winter turned into spring, Earla's mother and her younger sister, Gail flew out from Cambridge, Massachusetts to spend a couple of weeks with us, and of course, we showed them Hollywood, the La Brea Tar Pits and even took them to Disneyland. The two weeks passed swiftly and almost before we realized it, I was on Lincoln Blvd. driving them back to the airport. Earla was sad to see them go but was happier that they had visited.

Throughout this time and through the summer months, Chet would drop by the house and we'd sit down and run through different tunes in order to keep his chops up. At other times, I'd drive down to Redondo Beach to visit with him, Carol and the kids. I also kept myself busy teaching acting classes, an occasional gig with Phil Moore III and painting houses, including the homes of movie stars, directors, screenwriters and producers I'd meet through Nicky Blair at Stefanino's. In the fall of 1969, I got a call from one such producer that finally gave me hope of building another opportunity for Chet.

The producer was Jim Aubrey, who I'd known for a little over a year and who was soon to become head of MGM Studios. He asked me to meet him at the new house he'd recently purchased. He wanted a paint job completed for both the interior and exterior. The house once belonged to Liz Taylor when she was married to Eddie Fisher. Jim wanted to know if I'd be available to start the job right away because he had to fly to New York City to take on his duties as the new president of MGM Studios. I gave him an estimate and told him I'd start in a couple of days. He gave me a blank check and the keys to the house and the private telephone numbers to his offices at MGM in New York and Culver City.

I was excited for two reasons. One, I was going to be making some really good money for the paint job. And two, it meant that I would be in a great position to talk to Jim about the possibility of getting Chet a future record contract at MGM Records.

The weekend after Jim's call, I started working on the house, doing the exterior first. I was a very fast painter and it only took me two and a half days to paint the whole outside of the house. By Monday morning, I was inside painting the kitchen. Sometime later that afternoon, a very buoyant Jim walked into the house, having just flown in from New York City. He was now the official president of MGM Studios. I stopped what I was painting and congratulated him. He asked how things were going with the job, and I assured him everything was cool. He invited me to have dinner with him and Nicky Blair at Stefanino's later that night because he wanted to go over some of the colors he wanted for each room. I, of course, accepted his invitation. He left the house and I put all the painting equipment away, cleaned up and went home.

I was excited to tell Earla about the important meeting I had that night, and how I planned on talking about the possibility of getting a record contract for Chet. I took a shave and shower, put on some nice clothes and sat down with the kids to share some of the things that took place in their day. Each one told me about the projects they were working on, and before I realized, it was almost seven o'clock. I explained to them that Daddy had an appointment and wouldn't be able to play Monopoly with them that night, but probably would the next day.

The dinner with Jim Aubrey, Nicky Blair and I went along smoothly. Later on, we sat around drinking wine and celebrating Jim's new appointment. After a few glasses of wine I figured everyone would be in a more relaxed and favorable mood, so decided to test the waters and bring up Chet's name. I told both Nicky and Jim all about how hard Chet had been working to reshape his chops and the pain and agony he had gone through in order to learn how to play again. I told Jim how desperately scared Chet was of not being able to find more work as a musician in order to support his wife and three kids.

Jim was very nice and understanding of the whole situation and told me he would see what he could do. "I can't really promise you anything, Artt. But I'll see what I can do to help."

"Thanks a million, Jim. I really appreciate it."

We had more wine and Jim began talking to Nicky about the plans he'd be making at the studio in the next week, like bringing in new 'suits' to each department, and how Mike Curb had taken over as president of MGM Records. I didn't know too much about Mike Curb, but knew he was a young man who had become famous and successful during the mid-sixties leading a vocal group called "The Mike Curb Congregation" to worldwide fame. Almost as soon as Jim mentioned Mike's name, I had the idea to ask him if he'd have a talk with Mike about Chet. He said he would and get back to me sometime in the next few days while I was painting his house. I thanked him for the dinner and for his kindness and understanding toward Chet.

The next day, I arrived at Jim's house with the new paint colors I'd picked up at the Hollywood Sherwin William's store. I spread the drop-cloths on the master bedroom floor, and began to stir the paint. Jim walked in just as I finished. I guess he wanted to check how things were going. After we discussed what room he wanted me to do next, I asked him if he'd had a chance to speak to Mike Curb about Chet. He let me know that he would be seeing Mike later that day at a meeting he was holding at the studio. All the heads of every department would be present and after the meeting he would speak to Mike about the prospects of recording Chet. That was very good and promising news.

I went to work and finished the master bedroom and a guest bedroom before noon. After lunch I spent the rest of the day painting, happy and excited about the possibility of Chet getting a recording contract with MGM. Before I left for the day, I knocked off another bedroom, and two big clothes closets. I worked fast that day. I was tired and looking forward to having a good supper and then maybe going up to Nicky's restaurant to find out if he'd heard any news from Jim or Mike Curb.

I arrived at Stefanino's around 8:30 p.m. That was the time of night most of the big stars arrived. It was often like a Who's Who of entertainment any night at Stefanino's, with big names from Frank Sinatra to Steve McQueen, or Angie Dickenson, Anthony Quinn, Clint Eastwood, Sonny & Cher, Hollywood gossip columnist, Rona Barrett, you name it.

Once inside the restaurant, I went to talk with Pia, the hat/coat check girl. She was a handsome Italian lady in her early 30's, and had only been in the country for a little over two years, and still spoke with a heavy accent. I liked talking to her because she was always warm and sincere, and also because every big name that came into the restaurant had to come to her station to have their items checked. It was very entertaining for me to have the opportunity of being able to say hello to each of them. Of course, I had met the majority of the celebrities through Nicky and had also painted the houses of quite a few of them.

I hadn't been talking to Pia for more than ten minutes when in walked Jim Aubrey with a neatly dressed, good-looking young man in his 20's. Jim spots me talking to Pia and immediately comes over to say hello, and to introduce me to Mike Curb. He told Mike I was the one painting his house, and the one he's been talking to about Chet Baker. Mike and I shook hands and exchanged greetings. Jim asked if I had eaten yet, and if I'd like to join him and Mike for dinner. I thanked him for the offer and told him I had already eaten at home, but would be very happy to join them after their meal. Jim asked if Nicky was in the restaurant. He wasn't, but would be back shortly. Jim let me know Nicky could find them in the La Rosa Room when he arrived.

After Jim and Mike were shown to their table, I sat started talking to Pia again, and within a few seconds, one of the waiters came over and said that I had a phone call. It was Chet, asking me to come pick him up in Redondo Beach and drive him to some doctor's house.

I explained to him that I really couldn't leave at that particular time because I'd be meeting with Jim Aubrey, Mike Curb, and Nicky Blair about trying to negotiate a recording contract for him at MGM Records. I told him I'd come down to see him the following day to fill him in on the happenings. He was very happy about what I was trying to do for him, and hoped I could convince them to give him a chance. I went back to resume my conversation with Pia. A few minutes later Nicky walked in with Angel and I directed him to Jim and Mike in the La Rosa room, and quietly asked Nicky to put in a couple of good words about Chet. Nicky assured me that he would, and we left it at that.

About an hour later, I was seated at one of the large tables in the Bar section of the restaurant, in conversation with Pervis Atkins, a very strong and handsome man who was once a professional football player. He then became an agent for performers like the late David Carradine, singer and film star, Diahann Carroll, and others. We were always friendly with each other. As I sat there, I couldn't help but think to myself how beautiful Diahann was. I mean she was absolutely gorgeous. Nicky came over to the table and told me that Jim Aubrey and Mike Curb wanted me to join them at their table. When he said that all the guys at the table started to rib me, wondering how I could be invited to the president of MGM's table. I just ribbed them back and said that Jim recognized star quality when he saw it. We all had a good laugh at that one.

I followed Nicky to where we joined Jim and Mike Curb. Mo, the headwaiter, came to the table and Nicky asked him to serve us coffee and some of his mother's famous homemade Italian cookies, which were well loved by everyone who frequented the restaurant. I was more than a little on edge being in the company of these two major executives, but knew in my heart that this was the right moment. I began the conversation by asking Mike if he would consider signing Chet to do an album on the MGM label. He looked briefly at Jim, then at me, and I could see he was giving thought to my question. I explained a little about Chet's current situation, and Mike nodded. I figured that, being the president of a prestigious record company such as MGM, he would have been aware of Chet's reputation for drug use, and was probably being cautious. I assured him that Chet was straight and had been for months, and that all he'd been taking was synthetics and pain pills. I also told him about the successful, extended gig we'd done earlier that year at The Melody Room.

"All he needs is a break, Mike. I know Chet's made some

mistakes and has gotten himself into a few scrapes, but none of that has ever taken away from his God-given ability to play. That's still in him," I said with firm conviction. I also told Mike that it was my opinion that a lot of the other great jazz names had taken drugs over the years, but for some reason, the law decided to make an example of Chet Baker. I think it was because of all the adverse publicity he'd received when he was in Italy. It seemed that Chet was taking the brunt and blame for just about every major jazz musician out there who had ever taken drugs. And it wasn't fair.

"Chet's still a major name, Mike," I continued. "And he still has a lot of fans all over the world."

Mike said he knew and realized that was true. He exchanged a brief look with Jim, and then told me he would think about it for the next few weeks to see what kind of ideas popped into his head, and get back to me through Jim. I thanked him and reached my hand across the table to shake his hand and then Jim's. I got up, excused myself, walked over to Nicky, gave him a tap on the shoulder, and bent over to kiss Angel on the cheek. I left the restaurant in a real upbeat mood believing I had scored a few good points with young Mike Curb, and now, all I had to do was to be patient and wait until he called.

Chapter 30
Blood, Chet & Tears

The following Monday Nicky Blair called to let me know Jim Aubrey and Mike Curb would be coming to his restaurant later that night. He felt I should be there. I told him I would. I was so excited I jumped into my car and drove out to Redondo Beach to let Chet and Carol know. They were still without a phone and I knew they would be as excited as I was. I didn't stay too long because I wanted to make sure I had enough time to get home, shave, shower, get dressed and make it up to Stefanino's before 7 p.m.

Speaking with Mike that night, he told me that he was very interested in a project centered around Chet and his style of playing.

"Does that mean you're going to give Chet a recording contract?" He said it did. When he said that, it was all I could do to keep from jumping out of my chair and joyfully slapping him on the back, but I cooled it and maintained my composure.

Mike talked about how he had been doing a lot of thinking about a promotional angle geared toward the younger generation. Teen-age kids and young adults loved rock music and one group they really loved was 'Blood, Sweat & Tears.' I believe Mike had been thinking about having Chet cut an album playing their music but in his own jazz style, and in that way, both the record company and Chet would be able to reach a far wider group of listeners.

"In other words, Chet wouldn't actually be playing rock music as such. He'd retain his own jazz voice and identity, and blend it together with today's style of rock/jazz music and make an album, is that right?"

Mike told me that had been the original concept behind his whole idea of having Chet do the album. Chet would play the way he always had; only he'd be playing the exact same tunes from the "Blood, Sweat & Tears" album. He planned to get the same producer/arranger, Jerry Styner, for the album project. I asked him what would he call it.

"Blood, Chet & Tears," he said simply. He also wanted me to write the liner notes. He asked me to get in touch with Chet and run the whole idea and conversation we'd had by him. If Chet liked the idea and concept, to call him back and he'd set up a meeting, a contract and recording date. I thanked him very much for giving Chet an opportunity then excused myself and left the restaurant.

On my drive back home I found I wasn't really all that happy about the idea of Chet having to play rock-oriented music. On the other hand, it was clearly too good an offer to turn away from. There were no other record companies stepping up to make any offers to Chet. I knew Chet would more than likely be disappointed by the idea of having to play the music of Blood, Sweat & Tears, but at least he was being given a new chance and, hopefully, a new beginning that would lead to greater things.

The next day I drove to Chet's house to give him the news. When I walked in, he was seated on the couch half asleep. Carol was at the table drinking a cup of tea watching over the kids playing on the floor. I sat down next to him and asked why he looked so tired. He told me he'd had a rough morning and in a lot of pain. Carol assured me that Chet had only taken a few painkillers and that was the reason he was lethargic.

I breathed a sigh of relief and laid the news on him about Mike Curb's idea for the album. Chet reacted just as I thought he would. He wasn't real happy with the prospect playing that kind of music in order to get himself back into the recording end of the business. But I made him see the proverbial light at the end of his own dark tunnel.

"Man, think about it, Chet. You turn down a chance to record for a major label like Verve you might just as well kiss whatever career you have left goodbye! Think about it man... so you play a bunch of rock tunes by 'Blood, Sweat & Tears,' so what? They're a world famous group, and with you playing their music, it might just do more to help you than it can hurt you.

Besides, no matter what the music is, it's still going to be YOU playing jazz and improvising in your own way and style. Who gives a fuck what people might say? You guys can use the bread." He opened his eyes and just sort of stared at me contemplatively for a few seconds, then turned and looked over to Carol.

"Well… what do you think, Carol?

Carol told Chet she knew how much it bothered him to have to play rock arrangements and all, but also made the point that he'd still be playing in his own style, and that would make a difference. She also hinted that they could use the money to buy clothes and shoes for the kids, and some other things. She went on to say that whatever choice he made would be all right with her.

"Well, I really don't have any other offers," he said wearily. "So… maybe you'd better go ahead and set up the deal, Artt. I'll do it."

"That's great, Chet. I'll call Mike later today and set up the appointment for us." He seemed pleased with that. I wound up spending another hour with the two of them until the effects of the painkillers had worn off and he'd returned to his normal self. We talked about what the future might hold for Chet and his playing career, and about the possibility of their re-locating to New York City one day. It was Chet's feeling that he would be able to find more work on the East Coast than he could in L.A.

Paul, their youngest son, left his brother Dean and his sister, Melissa, (Missy) on the floor and walked directly over to Carol and asked if they could go outside into the backyard to play until dinnertime. She told them they could and the three of them whizzed by me like bees coming back from a pollen run. Carol asked if I could stay and have dinner with them, but I wanted to make it home in time to call Mike Curb and set up the meeting for the next day.

Chet got up and hugged me hard and thanked me, and Carol did likewise. I opened the sliding patio door and said goodbye to the kids, then left the house, happy that I had convinced Chet to do the album knowing that once he signed the contract, he'd be getting a decent amount of well needed bread.

The following afternoon, Chet and I met at my house and

drove the few blocks to MGM Studios to meet with Mike Curb. We entered Mike's office and seated ourselves close by his desk. I remained silent while he and Chet discussed plans for the upcoming album and terms of the record contract. The meeting was very cordial and went off without a hitch. Chet was happy and so was Mike. Chet signed several sheets of paper and then Mike handed him a check and the two reached across the desk and shook hands.

Chet was informed that the recording date would take place in the spring at the Sun-West Recording Studios on Sunset Boulevard in Hollywood. Mike told him that all the lead-sheets would be sent to him by mail and that he could use the next few months to familiarize himself with all the charts and arrangements. Chet smiled, nodded and shook Mike's hand again. We left the building and walked around back to the parking lot. Chet studied the amount on the check for a few moments, and then turned to me.

"I'm giving half of this to you for all you've done for me, Artt," he said.

"Oh no you're not, man! That's all for you, Carol and the kids, man."

He stopped walking and looked at me for a few seconds, puzzled.

"I dig you want to share the bread with me and all, Chet, but that's not what it's about. It's about you, and getting you back into the recording studio again."

"I really appreciate it, Artt... but calling the album, 'Blood, Chet & Tears'?" He stopped, rolled his eyes and shook his head in exaggerated distaste. "I don't know, man."

We started walking again until we reached my car and got in.

"Forget about the fucking title, Chet. In a way, it makes perfect sense. When you think about what you had to come through just to be able to play again, it really did take a lot of Blood, Chet & Tears."

He thought about that for a few seconds and his face exploded into a big smile. "That's what I want to see on your face, man, a smile. Let's go to Denny's and celebrate with a cheeseburger and coffee, what do you say?" He was all for that.

Chapter 31
A New Year

For the next few months of 1969 and into the New Year of 1970, Chet would try to make it to my house whenever he could so we could run through different tunes. My drums were set up in the den and I would always use brushes with him so he wouldn't have to use as much strength to push the air through. This, he said, helped him to develop lip strength and softer tone and also allowed him to maintain his endurance. He sounded just beautiful. He was well on his way back now because he was playing things I hadn't heard him play before.

We'd do bright-tempo tunes, medium tempos, blues and ballads and I'd still use brushes rather than sticks. It was during this time that I began to notice yet another difference in his sound and tone. His playing was darker, melancholic, and far more introspective, and he was working mostly in the lower register. I really loved it, and wondered if it was a natural evolution of his style as he adjusted to his embouchure challenges, or if it was the natural outcome of him becoming a more mature player.

Whatever it was, his sound, tone and phrasing had changed, and he had become a different player. I really couldn't put it into words except to say that he was able to make the trumpet sound like a flute and also like he was playing through a Harmon mute, an aluminum device some musicians used to alter the timbre and volume. Chet was able to make the kind of high-pitched buzz you could get from a mute, when he wasn't using one. I mean you were actually able to hear the flow of air going through the horn in addition to the tone itself. That's how soft, velvet and wispy it was. And the sound didn't change even when he played up-tempo, or when he placed the bell of the horn directly into the microphone. I remember asking him about the new sound and tone during one of our coffee and cigarette breaks. He said he'd discovered it while trying to build the three different embouchures.

"I was mainly trying to find a new way to play, so I continued to play all the tunes, like we're doing here, and a few weeks ago I finally got the sound I'd been hearing in my mind for months," he said happily. "And once I heard it, I knew that was the sound I wanted." His tone was more emotional and he was shaping the tones in a very expressive way that set him apart from any other horn player I'd ever heard. It was a breakthrough for him and that's why I could never understand the critics that said Chet was at his peak in the 1950's. I guess they weren't really listening beyond the surface of the music to how and what he was expressing from within.

I was really happy he had found something that brought joy to his heart rather than pain. He had been trying so hard, and now, he'd finally captured 'the special sound' that had been going around in his brain since he first picked up his horn so many months ago. It was as though he had been reborn.

He was determined to get back what had so brutally been taken away from him. And though he had achieved the near impossible, being able to play again, he wasn't about to stop there. He wanted more and more, and so he'd play, play and play until he was capable of playing whatever he wanted to, whenever he wanted to. It was not only amazing but also miraculous, because he was actually able to play just about any tune at any tempo without dropping off a tone. Also quite astonishing was the fact he had somehow found a way to develop three different embouchures, one in the center, and on the left and right sides of his mouth, unusual to say the least. He also played muted a lot when practicing because he said it helped build up his playing strength and breathing. This, he explained, allowed him to play for lengthier periods, but there'd be times when he'd have to stop completely, due to the intense pain or numbness around his cheeks and jaw.

I got to know his playing so well I could almost feel where he was going melodically as soon as he played a note or phrase, and this always amazed him. Chet was living proof of that great quote made by Bird: "*If you haven't lived it, there's no way you can play it.*" Chet sure lived it and he was sure able to play it.

Speaking of Charlie Parker, Chet once spoke to me about something he'd been told by a couple musicians who were outside the Tiffany Club after his first audition with Bird. Chet had done something Bird had personally never heard any other player ever do before, and that was to play back note for note the exact solo that Bird himself had just finished playing. Bird had been amazed by Chet's uncanny ability to have the kind of ears to do such a thing. The late, great tenor saxophonist and fellow band-mate of Chet, Phil Urso, also confirmed this statement to me.

I told Chet that I completely agreed with what Bird had said, and also what I would later come to learn Gerry Mulligan had to say about Chet. He felt Chet had the fastest reflex time and response between brain and fingers than any other musician he'd ever seen or heard. In my humble opinion, Chet also had the biggest ears of any horn player on earth because most players would have to hear a solo a few times over in order to transcribe it. But Chet could hear it once and play it on the spot. Truly uncanny! And what was extraordinary about the whole idea is that he really didn't know what he was doing technically. I personally believe that along with Chet's beautiful sound and tone, was his innate, God-gifted ability to compose on the spot.

Chapter 32
Recording Again

In the spring of 1970, an executive from MGM Records called me to set Chet's recording date for the following week. He was to be at the Sun-West Recording Studio in Hollywood at 10:00 am. I called Chet's mother at the W.T. Grant store where she worked, and asked her to give Chet the news and for him to call me about the details. Vera was very excited and assured me she'd tell him everything I'd said.

On the day of the recording session, Chet was at my house before 7:30 am. He was excited, but pissed, and ready to get it over with. He was not the least bit happy about having to record that music, but excited about his being able to make the money he and Carol needed. He didn't say much, and I wasn't about to prod him. During the drive, Chet was edgy and didn't say a word until I pulled up in front of the recording studio.

"I really don't like having to do this album, man. I really don't. I know how hard you worked to make it all happen, and I appreciate everything you've done Artt, but I just don't feel good about having to play that fucking kind of shit, you know?"

He went on a verbal tirade about rock music, how it had nothing to say, that it was a sojourn into nothingness that had taken over the country, the record industry, and most of the good paying club gigs. He talked about how the rock musicians were making the heavy bread while great jazz musicians had to work for scale or less. The thing that pissed him off the most and found the most unfair, was that just about every one of the rock musicians smoked pot, popped pills and mainlined heroin, but society just seemed to turn their backs on it all. He couldn't understand it.

I agreed with him completely, but also reminded him that Mike Curb had gone out on a limb to make this recording date possible for him. I suggested he just go into the studio, record the thing, and be done with it. He didn't say a word for almost two minutes, then turned and smiled.

"You're right, man," he agreed.

We went inside to the front office and were immediately greeted by sound engineer, Donn Landee, and producer/musical director for the album, Jerry Styner. A huge ceiling to floor sound proof, plate glass window separated the office from the recording studio, and on the other side, a group of musicians were looking out toward us. As soon as they spotted Chet, they left and came running out. After the introductions, Chet wanted to get right to the business at hand and let Jerry know it, but in a nice way. Jerry got the musicians back into the studio and directed Chet to a high back leather chair off to the side of the musicians. I recognized some of them, like Joe Pass, Buddy Collette and drummer Hal Blaine.

Chet wanted me to be in the same room with him but I made the excuse that I was nursing a headache and would be just outside in the outer office watching. Jerry got things under way and the first tune they did was *Easy Come, Easy Go*. I couldn't stand it. I could only imagine what Chet was going through. They finished that one and did another called *Sugar, Sugar*, and when that was finished, Chet did a Beatle's tune called *Something*, which he sang. To my surprise, it sounded pretty damned good. After that, they did four more tunes, with Chet singing again on the song *Come Saturday Morning*. Again, he sounded great. They played two more tunes, and the recording session was over.

Chet and I went into the engineer's room and listened to the playbacks together. A young graphic artist, Laura Thompson, had been drawing Chet while he played and handed him the finished piece, which Mike wound up using for the front and back covers of the album. Jerry Styner and Donn Landee were both completely satisfied with the outcome of the takes, so we split.

Chet was really grateful to Mike Curb for giving him an opportunity to record again. He told me he liked Mike and felt he was 'an honest cat who knew what was happenin.' He referred to Jim Aubrey as someone he looked up to and respected. And for Chet to say something like that was pretty impressive because he just didn't give compliments away unless he really meant it.

He was, however, relieved that it was over with. He thought he had played well and was satisfied with his singing of *Something*, a song written by George Harrison of the Beatles, and *Come Saturday Morning*, made popular by The Sandpipers and written by Fred Karlin and Dory Previn. But Chet didn't ever want to have to play that kind of music again. That night, I took Earla, Chet and Carol out to Stefanino's to celebrate. We had Chateaubriand ala Bouquetiere and Beaujolais wine. Everything was delicious and more expensive than I expected. But thank God Nicky covered half the tab for me, which was great. On the way back home, I was driving south on La Cienega, and just as I crossed Beverly Boulevard, Chet suddenly became sick and wanted me to stop and pull over as fast as I could. I pulled out of traffic and over to the curb and as soon as I did, he opened the rear door, stuck his head outside and heaved up the delicious meal he'd just eaten. He'd tell me later on that he felt he had prostituted himself and he couldn't take it.

Chapter 33
Doctor's Orders

A day or two later, I got a call from Chet that he was having trouble with his car and asked if I could pick him up the next day and take him to his doctor's office. He was having a rough time and needed a refill of painkillers. When I arrived the next day, around noon, Chet was seated on the couch rubbing his cheek and jaw in obvious pain. He'd apparently taken the last of his pain pills the night before because there were none to be found anywhere. We left immediately for the doctor's.

I drove up in front of a house that Chet said was his doctor's and parked. It looked like a decent area with other nice looking homes and well-kept lawns. I looked around and noticed a business sign but couldn't make out a name because of where I'd parked. I had no reason to wonder and just figured it was his doctor and he was conducting his practice out of his home like a lot of other doctors did. Chet wanted me to go in with him, but I told him I'd wait in the car rather than sit in a stuffy waiting room. He left and went inside. I lit up a cigarette and tuned the radio to KBCA- FM and just sat there listening to some great jazz. Every now and then I'd take a look up to the doctor's office door, and it suddenly hit me that there were no people going in or coming out to the office, which was pretty strange. But, I shrugged it off and immersed my mind in the music.

I wasn't aware how much time had gone by before I saw a very agitated Chet come busting out of the doctor's office, moving toward the car like an arrow shot out of a bow. He opened the door, jumped in, and told me to take off. I didn't hesitate.

Chet started going on about how his regular doctor hadn't been there, and how the other doctor standing in for him had come on to him.

"You gotta be kidding me! How do you know for sure, I

mean, what'd he do?"

He related how when he opened the door and went into the waiting room area, the first thing he noticed was the smell of fresh paint, and a different doctor. He asked where the regular doctor was, and was told he was on vacation and wouldn't be back for two weeks. He told the new doctor he was in a lot of pain and needed a prescription for painkillers immediately. The doctor asked Chet to follow him into his office, and as soon as they were in there, instead of writing out a prescription, the doctor concerned himself with showing Chet how the office had just been redecorated, complete with a new glass enclosed shower, and wanted Chet to be the first to try it out.

"You're in pain, and he's trying to get you to take a shower?" I asked, finding the suggestion so humorous I had to laugh because it was so unexpected. It wasn't funny to Chet though because he was pissed and had a real mean look in his eyes. "So what'd you do?" I asked.

"I told him I hadn't come to look at a fucking paint job, but needed a prescription for pain." Chet said the doctor ignored what he said and told him that he was too tense, and should take a warm shower immediately to help calm his nerves. "I knew then that the cat was coming on to me, but didn't say anything because I needed the script." He said the next thing he knew, the guy was standing right behind him, and then felt a hand on the side of his leg. He said he turned around and slapped the cat across the face so hard he hit the wall and fell back on his ass.

Chet said the doctor was afraid and very concerned and apologized like crazy, telling Chet he didn't know what had come over him. He was terribly sorry and asked Chet not to report him to the medical board.

"I told him I was going to report him, and he pleaded with me not to, telling me again and again how sorry he was," Chet said. Then he told the doctor to write him a prescription and he wouldn't report him. While the doctor sat at his desk writing out the prescription, Chet said he grabbed a prescription pad off another desk and stuffed it into his pocket. "Now I'll be able to write out my own scripts," he said and casually lit up a cigarette.

I asked him how in hell he was going to be able to do that and he held up the written prescription, and said he'd just copy this guy's signature. I was really concerned about the prospects of him getting caught, and the possibility of the doctor calling the police to report him. He was as cool as a cucumber and merely shrugged it off with an air of confidence.

"He won't man... because he knows if he did, I'd report him to the medical board and they'd run his ass out of the state." Chet didn't actually hate homosexuals as such. He just didn't like anyone getting too familiar by putting their hands on him, be it male or female.

He asked me to stop at a drug store he had frequented before. While he was inside, I sat in the car contemplating all the bad things that could and probably would happen to him if he ever got caught forging a doctor's name in order to cash a script. The thought scared the hell out of me, but it didn't appear to bother Chet. A few minutes later, he came out of the pharmacy, got into the car and I drove him home.

One night, a week or so later, after Earla and I had just placed the kids in bed, I was sitting in my favorite chair watching television. Earla was putting the finishing touches to her 'Angel gown,' designed for Angel Tompkins. The phone rang and I got to it quickly so it wouldn't wake the kids. It was Carol, and she was distraught. The police had arrested Chet. They'd be taking him to the L.A. County jail downtown where he'd have to stay until his court date. She was very concerned for his safety, because she'd heard from others that County jail was worse than it was at the Lincoln Heights jail.

"Oh, Carol, I pray to God he doesn't have to do time in prison," I said anxiously, and asked what he had done. Sure enough, he had forged some doctor's name, and tried to have the prescription filled. She gave me the telephone number of the County jail and asked me to call them and ask if it would be all right for me to visit Chet as she wasn't able to leave the children. I assured her I would.

I hung up and called the County jail, explaining who I was and if I could visit Chet in place of his wife because she was unable to leave her three children. He asked me a couple questions and told me I could see him on the following afternoon. Carol called back and I told her I had been cleared to visit with Chet and she felt completely relieved.

The following morning I got a telephone call from Chet's mom, wanting to know if she could come along when I went to visit Chet. I, of course, told her she could. The visiting hours were from 2 pm to 4 pm, so I asked her to meet me at my house, as it would be easier for us to leave from Culver City. She happily agreed and was at my house a little before noon. When we arrived at County, we were led to the visiting area and informed that only one of us would be allowed to visit at a time. It would be better for Vera to spend the first hour with him, so I waited in the visitor's area.

There were several other men and women in the visitor's area, all waiting their turn to visit their loved ones or friends. There were no signs saying that we couldn't smoke, so I lit up a cigarette and started to pace the room, my mind flooded with thoughts about what might happen to Chet. Would he be sent to jail or prison? And if so, what would Carol and the kids do? How would they be able to get along? How would they be able to survive? I was really troubled, and at the same time, royally pissed, especially in view of the record release coming up.

I was so wrapped up in my thoughts, I was totally unaware an hour had gone by and Vera was standing in front of me.

"How'd it go in there? How's he doing, Vera?" She looked like she was going to cry and I put my arms around her for a hug. I led her over to a chair at the far end of the room. I could see the glistening in her soft blue eyes as she looked up at me.

"He's doing all right, Artt, and he's really looking forward to seeing you."

Knowing she'd be fine, I went in to visit with Chet. I walked into a long narrow room where there were a number of cubicles and a single chair placed directly in front of a thick, plate-glass window. There was a small desktop upon which rested a black telephone. I sat down and looked on the other side of the plate glass and saw another black telephone. Within seconds Chet entered on the other side of the glass and sat down opposite me. He gestured for me to pick up the receiver. I quickly did and put it to my ear.

"Thanks for coming, Artt, and thanks for bringing my mother."

"What's going on, what's going to happen?"

"Well… they busted me for cashing a script. Either the pharmacist or some auditor noticed a difference in the handwriting on the scripts, got suspicious and called the doctor's office to check it out."

"You think it was that doctor you stole that prescription pad from that turned you in?"

"No… no… I don't believe he would've done that," he said with confidence, and explained what he thought might have happened. Every drug store in L.A. County was audited every few months, and that some eagle-eyed auditor must have noticed that some of the signatures were not quite the same, and put two and two together.

"But how could they trace it to you, I don't get it?"

"Well… I guess when they were checking the scripts the doctors had written for me against the ones I'd written and…" He stopped, and shrugged his shoulders in that proverbial 'I don't know' manner.

"Oh, man, you mean they've got more than one forged script?" He lowered his head as if ashamed and nodded. "Oh, Chet. What's the worst they can do for something like that?"

"Well... with my reputation?" He shook his head, shrugged and looked at me discouraged. "I don't really know, Artt… It all depends on the judge."

I told him how worried Carol and his mother were, and how much the kids missed him. I also let him know that I was worried, too.

"Listen to me, Chet, you're almost forty years old, and what are you doing? You're sitting in County jail for forging a script just so you could get a few extra pain pills! You've got to wake up turn your life around, man! You've got Carol, your kids, your mother, your music, and me, too, man!"

"I know, man… I know," he said solemnly. I could almost see the wheels of reason spinning around in his head. He looked directly at me with those piercing eyes and I got the feeling that my words had reached his heart. We spoke of future plans and before we knew it, the hour had flown by and I had to leave. I assured him I'd be back to see him the following day, and with sad reluctance, left and went to rejoin Vera.

The following morning a letter was delivered from the state

of California, Department of Corrections stating that Chet had solely named me for a character reference, and as such, was asked a series of questions about him. I answered them to the best of my ability and sent the form back.

Later that afternoon, I went by myself to visit Chet again and mentioned that I'd received a questionnaire character reference form the state regarding him. I asked if he knew anything about it. He thought maybe the system felt it would be better to have a close friend evaluate his personality and character traits. His reasoning was that I'd be less prone to show partiality, rather than Carol or his mother, and that might go over more favorably for him with the presiding judge. It made sense to me, and it also filled my heart and soul to think that Chet loved and trusted me enough to name me as the only person he wanted as his character witness.

On my next visit to see Chet, he informed me that his trial date had been set for the next day. I told him I would pray that God would provide a judge that would show him understanding and leniency. All I could do after that was wait for the outcome. When I got home I told my wife about the trial date and called Vera at work and told her. We talked for a minute or so and she confessed how worried she was about him. She started to cry softly. I comforted her and told her to have faith and be strong for Carol and the kids' sake. She composed herself and told me she would call me the following day.

After a long night of broken sleep, I got up around noon, made myself a cup of instant coffee and watched my sweet three year old daughter, Kathy play with her little dolls. Earla was at the counter modeling something from a big ball of clay. She was not only a seriously fine jazz vocalist and dress designer, but also a gifted sculptor and visual artist, as well.

I had finished my breakfast of English muffins and coffee when the phone rang. I lifted the receiver and said an anxious hello. The bittersweet voice of Chet's mother was on the other end. Vera had just come from the courtroom. She was happy the judge had been fair and kind. He'd been a fan of Chet's since law school, and even had some of Chet's records.

"That's great, Vera, but what happened? Does Chet have to go to a federal prison or what?"

"No, thank God!" she answered with great sigh of relief. "The judge could have given him five years, but was sympathetic, and felt Chet wouldn't get the kind of help he needed doing hard time. He sentenced him to 90 days at Chino for drug rehabilitation. Isn't that great, Artt?"

When I heard that I thanked God for having heard and answered my prayers.

Chet had included me on the list of his family members allowed to visit during his 90 days at Chino. Two days later I drove out. He seemed really happy to see me and told me about the strict methadone rehabilitation program they'd put him on. He was upbeat about it. I remembered him mentioning methadone the day I'd taken him to the house near MacArthur Park. He obviously knew a lot about the medicine now and felt very strongly that it was going to help him.

He asked how Carol and the kids were doing, and I said they were doing fine, but missed him terribly. He looked so sad, yet managed to smile. I asked if there was anything he needed, like shaving cream or aftershave lotion, and he said no, he was cool in that department. We lit a cigarette and before I had the chance to finish smoking it, the visiting hours were over and I had to leave. I told him I'd come back in a couple of days.

"It'd be a lot easier to write letters, and lot cheaper too, man," he said, and thanked me for taking the time to come and visit him. He mentioned that it was important for him to know I was there for him. "I really value your friendship, man," he said and smiled that boyish smile.

"And I value yours, too, Chet. I hate like hell to leave without you," I said. He shrugged, and said the remaining 80 days would go by pretty fast, and before I knew it, he'd be knocking on my door. We hugged each other for a few moments, and I assured him I'd check in on Carol and the kids several times a week to make sure they were all right, and left. Walking away, I couldn't help but turn around a couple of times to look back and wave to him.

Outside, I got into my car, jumped on the freeway and made my way back home praying that God would watch over Chet while he was there, and when released, Chet would want to go straight and no longer have a desire for heroin. All I could do now was hope, wait, and wonder about the word, Methadone.

True to my word, I continued to check in with Carol and the kids every chance I could. And then, on a quiet day, I was in my backyard soaking up the sun and listening to Chet and me on my tape recorder, when I heard the excited little voice of my daughter, Kathy breaking through the music.

"Daddy, Daddy, Chet's here!" she cried out.

I sat up quickly and turned around. There stood Chet. I jumped up, hugged him and told him how happy I was to see him. Kathy, on seeing me embrace Chet, had this big smile of joy on her angelic face. Earla, sensing that Chet and I wanted to talk, took Kathy by the hand and led her inside.

Chet lit a cigarette, passed it to me and lit another for himself. I asked him how it had gone at Chino, and how he felt about being free again. He told me it felt good to be back on the street. He was glad the judge had taken into consideration he was married and had three kids.

"I had a lot of time to think… that's when I really started to think about all you had said to me, Artt. I do have a beautiful wife and three beautiful kids. Thank you for reminding me of that." He stopped talking, looked around the yard, then up into the vastness of the sky, and said how glad he was to be alive and free.

"I've really got to be cool though," he continued. "I can't afford to fuck up, you know?"

"What are you doing tonight?" I asked. "You wanna go to a club and sit in?"

He said he wanted to lay low for a while and spend time with Carol and the kids. And that's just what he did, much to Carol's delight.

Several weeks later, Chet came by the house. He had his trumpet with him and wanted to check out some club in L.A. He said he could probably sit in and blow a little. Well, I was all for that and asked Earla if she'd mind if I went along. She gave me the green light, and we split.

Chapter 34
A New Beginning

We found the jazz club he was talking about and went inside to check out the layout. There was a quintet playing and they sounded pretty good so we made our way to a table approximately fifty feet away from the small raised bandstand and sat down. Immediately, one of the musicians recognized Chet and gestured to the others, and they looked over excitedly. The leader, a piano player in his late 20s, ended the tune and reached for the microphone as the audience applauded lightly. The piano player looked into the audience and spoke into the microphone. He thanked them and mentioned that there was a very special jazz musician in the club, and felt that if the people gave the musician a warm round of applause, he might want to come up to the stand and play a couple of tunes with the group.

I jabbed Chet's arm excitedly with my elbow believing they were going to call him up to play. Chet obviously thought so also because he placed the trumpet case on the table and carefully removed the trumpet. He reached into his pants pocket and took out the mouthpiece and placed it into the neck of the horn and waited. But instead of introducing Chet, the man called up some younger trumpet player instead. As the young trumpeter made his way up to the stand, he looked over at Chet and gave him one of the proverbial, 'it's not my fault, man' kind of looks.

Chet shrugged and managed a weak smile, but I was burning inside.

"What's wrong with that fucking jerk, man?" I asked incredulously. "Can you believe that shit, Chet? That little prick ignoring you like that! Who the hell does this guy think he is?" I was burning and had all I could do to hold myself back from leaping out of my chair and slapping the living shit out of that smug little bastard.

"Well... it doesn't really matter Artt," he said softly. But the look on his face spoke volumes of his hurt and insult by the obvious snub. Yet, he never said a mean word about the clown. Instead, he lowered his head for a few moments and sat there quietly with only God knowing what turmoil he was going through. He raised his head, looked at me and managed a smile and put his mouthpiece back into his pocket, then carefully placed the horn into the trumpet case and put it on his lap out of sight.

I felt so bad for Chet. I felt like crying. I just couldn't figure the whole thing out. How could anyone possibly ignore a trumpet player of Chet Baker's magnitude? Yet, it was happening again before our very eyes. I asked Chet if he wanted to get out of there.

"No... I don't want the young player to think we don't like him... let's just wait 'til he's finished. Then we'll split," he said. Chet was so beautiful in that way. A person could put him down but he wouldn't necessarily retaliate. Often times, he chose to let things go by, like he did that night. He knew it wasn't the trumpeter's fault, and he sure as hell wasn't going to allow the self-inflated piano player to believe he had managed to hurt his feelings either. When the trumpet player ended his solo, Chet applauded him and the young man beamed from ear to ear with pride, raised his horn to Chet in admiration and respect. I still wanted to kick the piss out of the piano player though, but Chet told me to forget it... that it wasn't worth getting myself in trouble over.

"Let's cut out," he said.

So we stood up and left the club without saying a word to anyone. On the way home Chet was quite solemn. Yet another insensitive musician had hurt his feelings.

I was hurt, pissed and angry about the whole episode myself and wanted to know just what the hell it was going to take for Chet to be afforded the respect he rightfully deserved. It was beginning to border on the absolute ridiculous. Most of the working musicians were usually taking some kind of shit themselves, yet they were still being treated with reasonable kindness and respect, so why not Chet? I knew in my heart that Chet's time would come, and believe I caused him to also start having faith in that eventuality.

It was sometime in late summer 1970 and I was just finishing lunch with the family when the phone rang. Chet was on the other end and he didn't sound upbeat. He had something important to tell me, and asked if I could meet him at his house the next day. I had to finish a painting job at Nicky Blair's and asked if he could meet me there. He said he'd be there in the early afternoon.

The following day, around one o'clock, I'm standing outside Nicky's house having a smoke when Chet pulled up into the long driveway. His mother was with him. Chet got out, as I made my way over to him, waving to Vera, who remained in the car.

"What's happenin'? I asked. "You all right, man?" He nodded and said he was, but didn't explain further.

"Then what's going on?" I persisted. "Something wrong with Carol, or one of the kids?" He shook his head and finally told me his mother had been transferred to the W.T. Grant Store in the San Jose area. She'd already bought a nice ranch house in Milpitas, and that he, Carol and the kids would be moving up there with her. The kicker was that they'd be leaving the next day.

"Tomorrow!" I said, shocked. "Why? Why do you have to leave so soon, man?"

"Well, you know, man... I'm not really getting any work around L.A. to make enough bread to support my family or pay the rent. So, it'll probably be a lot better for me in the Frisco area, you know?" He paused and finally looked directly at me. "I'll miss you a lot, Artt," he said with a soft sadness. "We'll stay in touch with each other, and as soon as I get a gig I'll send for you."

It was a real difficult thing to say goodbye to Chet. We had come through so much together during the last two years. Our friendship had grown strong, as did our mutual trust. I knew they had a lot of packing to do and things to be arranged and readied for the long trip the following morning. As was our routine, we lit up a last cigarette and stood there smoking for a while. I finally broke the silence. "I'll always be here for you, Chet. Just a phone call away, man."

He nodded and smiled, "I know that, Artt, and I appreciate it. I'll be there for you, too man, you know that." He suggested I drive up with my family to spend a few days with him and Carol once they'd settled in. I told him it was a great idea and would look forward to getting his call. Vera, not wanting to be rude, called softly to Chet, telling them they needed to be leaving soon. He told her he'd be right over and let out a long sigh.

"C'mon," I said, "I'll walk you to the car so I can say my goodbyes to Vera."

When we got to the car, I went around to the passenger side, opened the door and gave Vera a warm hug and a kiss on the cheek. Her eyes glistening, she said she'd miss me, and I'd always be welcome in her home. I thanked her for that and for inviting Chet and his family to share her new place. I walked around to where Chet was standing and shook his hand, then we hugged each other. Man, I had all I could do to hold back my tears. Chet must have had a hard time, too, because he turned his head away from me and quickly slid in behind the wheel and started the car. I told him I loved him, to be careful and to make sure he called me the first chance he got. He said he loved me too and would call me within a week. He backed the car out of the yard. And I just stood there in Nicky's driveway feeling empty, as the car pulled away and disappeared around the corner. When it did, a door closed in my life and my heart dropped like a stone. I had no real idea if or when I'd see him again. All I could do was pray, and that's exactly what I did.

A few weeks later I got a phone call from Chet telling me that they were all doing fine. He said with a hint of pride in his voice that he'd been sticking to his Methadone program, had gained a few pounds, and was feeling pretty good. This was great news because it meant I wouldn't have to worry about him so much anymore.

I asked what the music scene was like in the Bay Area and if he was able to get many gigs there. He said it was just as slow there as it had been for him in L.A. He did say however, that he'd found a little jazz club in San Jose, and would make it there from time to time to sit in with local groups to keep his chops up in case a recording deal or club gig came along. He wanted to make sure he'd be ready for any eventuality.

Near the end of January 1971, Chet called and said he had a two-night gig in San Francisco and wanted me to play it with him. As happy and excited as I was to do it, I told him I couldn't. I'd already made a previous commitment to my daughter, Rhonda, that I'd be present when she received her Bluebird pin from the Girl Scouts. To her it was a very big moment, and I surely didn't want to break my promise. Chet totally understood and said he'd do the gig without a drummer, and call me on the weekend.

With Chet, Carol and the kids now safely living with his mother in northern California, I knew he was ready for a new start.

Epilogue

Now I figured it was time for me to try my luck at resurrecting my acting career, and was soon making the rounds to the major motion picture studio casting directors in the hopes of landing a part in a movie or television series.

Chet and I spoke often about the jazz scene up in the Bay Area. In one call, he didn't sound enthusiastic about his situation.

"Well… nothing's really been happening up here you know?" he said with an air of dismay. "So I'm thinking about running up to Denver to see Phil Urso. Carol and the kids can stay here with my mother for a couple weeks." He felt quite strongly he'd find work playing in Phil's group. I told him to make sure to let me know where he was and where he'd be going and when, so we could stay in touch. He assured me he would, and that's all I needed to hear.

I managed to book a part in a western starring Robert Conrad that would be filmed in Tucson, Arizona. I had worked once before with Bob in a bit part on his show "The Wild, Wild West" and was looking forward to being in one of his films. I called Chet and told him all about my good luck, and he was genuinely glad for me, and hoped I'd be able to get a lot more work in the movies. I asked if the music scene had changed for him up there yet, but nothing had. He and Carol had been talking about leaving Milpitas, if he couldn't find anything in Denver. I told him I thought it would be a great idea for him to make it to New York City. He was still a world famous name, and was playing better than ever, and without doubt, would get a gig with the first phone call. He told me he'd think it over and would call me when he reached a solid decision. I told him I loved him and looked forward to hearing from him.

For me, and my big movie role, one of the financial backers pulled out of the deal and the movie didn't get made. Earla, the kids and I had been in Tucson for several months, having left L.A. after the massive earthquake in February 1971. We had been staying at the Desert Inn Hotel with the rest of the production crew hoping Bob Conrad would be able to get more financing. But it didn't happen. There were a few very tense weeks for me, as the hotel was holding me liable for a very sizeable tab and I was down to less than $40. Without the salary from the planned movie, I was stuck. I'd put in a call to Chet and let him know what I was up against. I knew he wasn't in any shape to help me out financially; I just needed to talk to someone close, someone who had already gone through hell and come out alive. God bless him, Chet offered to sell his trumpet and send me whatever money he could get by Western Union.

When he said he'd sell his horn, it hit me straight in the heart. I assured him things would no doubt work out. He made me promise to call and let him know, and I made that promise.

Tommy Huff, the main stunt man, had been communicating with the hotel manager and Bob Conrad about the situation. To my great relief, he told me that Bob had covered the entire tab, which turned out to be over four thousand dollars. I shook my head in disbelief. When I told Earla the news, she was ecstatic and started to pack our clothes immediately. We left the hotel within the hour and began our long trek to Maine.

Bob Conrad had hardly known me, and yet he went to bat for me. On camera, he always portrayed the proverbial rough and tumble kind of guy, who would fight a giant to protect a friend. Well, for the record, he was precisely the same guy off camera. Bob Conrad has a heart as big as the state of Alaska and as warm as a summer's day. I'll never forget his kindness.

Once back in Maine, I called Chet and let him know what had happened and we were doing pretty good back in my hometown of Westbrook. I was in the process of buying my own home under the GI Bill, and would probably be moving within the month.

"When I get the house, I want you, Carol and the kids to make it up here to spend a few weeks with us because, man, you'd love this place," I said enthusiastically. He was genuinely happy that we'd be getting our own house, and that one day, he was going to surprise us.

Earla, the kids and I began to get settled into our new home. It was a cozy little two-bedroom house set on three and a half acres of lush green forest land. No one could build behind us, in front of us or to the side of us. It was an absolutely perfect spot for a musician and artist to live with three growing kids. I was back painting houses and making good money and it was good being home near family. Chet and I stayed in touch, speaking over the telephone and writing letters and holiday cards. By the end of October 1974, I realized that more than three years had gone by since I'd last seen Chet face-to-face.

I was sitting in my chair thinking about how quickly the time had flown by, when the phone rang and snapped me to my senses. It was Chet. He was in New York City and had recently finished cutting an album. Things were really beginning to look up for him. He said that while he was in Denver playing with Phil Urso he'd run into Dizzy Gillespie, who'd gotten him a gig in New York. He'd rented a house in the suburbs and sent for Carol and the kids, and couldn't wait to see us all again.

He also said he'd been asked to do a reunion concert with Gerry Mulligan at Carnegie Hall, but wasn't sure he really wanted to do it. He and Mulligan had a mutual dislike for each other, especially for Mulligan's attitude and ego.

"Fuck him and his ego, Chet," I said quickly. "And remember our first night at the Melody Room, what we set out to do, and how far you've come since then. Do the concert, man," I said emphatically. "And forget about the other bullshit." He didn't say anything, which I knew meant he was really giving it a lot of serious thought.

We talked for a while longer, in which time we made plans on how we'd be getting together again and when. I told him I felt late spring or early summer would the best time for all of us to get together because I had recently gotten over a battle with double pneumonia and didn't dare risk going to a major city like New York where there would be millions of germs.

"I got a great idea, Chet. Why don't you and Carol make plans to come up here to Maine in early summer and spend some time with us? It's lush and gorgeous, like the last frontier. You guys would love it." I went on to describe the tall pine trees, clean air, pure water, and plenty of fresh water lakes for the kids to swim in. The Atlantic Ocean was only a few miles from where we lived. "It would be a great place for Carol and kids to live while you're on the road on in Europe. And dig, it only takes about six hours to drive from here to the city. You can't beat it man! Hell, you could probably buy a house up here with a couple acres for about 45 thousand bucks, man."

"Well, it sure does sound nice, Artt. I'll give it a lot of thought."

It was great to know that Chet's career had begun to take off and that more work and recognition were coming his way.

The way things were working out caused me to remember a conversation I'd had with my father one afternoon in late June back in 1958. It was some six months after my son Arthur was born, and I was talking to my father about wanting to make a career in music, and what he thought my chances might be. We both felt that I had a good chance because at that time, the only other white Be Bop drummer that I personally knew of was, Stan Levey. I'd met Stan some eight years earlier at the Spot Light Lounge in New York City, and felt he would hip me to some group who might be looking for a good drummer.

My dad knew how much I wanted to play with Chet Baker ever since I'd met him in 1954 at Storyville in Boston. He brought up the fact of how hard it was going to be to bring up a family and go on the road. He told me it was going to be a very tough choice for me to make because he knew how much I loved playing drums, and how much I loved my wife and my son, and of the strong probability of our having other children in the future.

He reflected on his own life, and how very, very much he had wanted a career playing sax. He felt he could have become a name in the music world had he tried. He then said something to me that I will never forget.

"Zeke..." – he always called me that after the prophet Ezekiel because he somehow thought one day I'd be a man of the Bible – "It comes down to passion and responsibility. I had the heart and the passion to play and make a success of it, but I also had the responsibility of taking care of your mother and you seven kids."

He went on to say that during the Depression years and

World War II, there was really little or no chance for him to leave all of us and go out on the road. There just wasn't enough steady work for a musician except in the big bands, and that meant going on tour. So he said he made his choice. He chose responsibility over passion, and said he never once regretted it, because he'd succeeded in caring for all of us. He did admit though that there had been times when he wondered what it might have been like to be a full–time musician. But in the long run, he was always glad he'd made the choice that he did.

Passion. Responsibility. Success.

Chet had a passion for playing, and his music affected many people's lives, and obviously, my own. He was a completely honest player in that he didn't go for playing 'licks' or 'rehearsed phrasing.' What came out of Chet's horn was pure honesty and depth of heart. He gave his all on every tune regardless of who might be in the audience. He played good or great depending on how he felt at the time. He didn't try to please or impress anyone but himself. He once said to me that, if it sounded good to him, he figured it would have to sound good to his listeners as well. He was so focused on music that he gave his whole life over to it.

Throughout my life, I've had a passion for jazz. And I am grateful to have been so blessed to help Chet accomplish the near impossible: to play again, to get his comeback gig and a recording contract from a major label, and a whole new beginning.

And much like my father, I have always been glad I made the choice to love and support my family.

Passion. Responsibility. Success.

Now that I've been able to complete this book of memoirs, I feel I have achieved all three.

Artt Frank,
Green Valley, Arizona, 2013

End of Volume One

Coming Soon
Volume Two

Chet Baker:
The Man Behind the Horn

A Memoir
By

Artt Frank

About the Author

Artt Frank, bop drummer/composer, and author, is one of the few authentic bop musicians on the scene today. Born in the small paper mill town of Westbrook, Maine on March 9, 1933, Artt is best known for his long-term association with Chet Baker, with whom he collaborated for over 20 years. Artt has also been worked with an impressive list of jazz luminaries over the past sixty years including the great Charlie Parker, Tadd Dameron, Dexter Gordon, Sonny Stitt, Miles Davis, Bud Powell, Jimmy Heath, Al Cohn, Ted Curson, and many others, including one memorable night with the great singer, Billie Holiday

In 2004, Artt completed his book "Essentials for the Be Bop Drummer" with Pete Swan and published by Tim Schaffner, publisher (and drummer!) of Schaffner Press, Inc.

Artt Frank was inducted into the Oklahoma Jazz Hall of Fame in November, 2010.

He currently lives in Green Valley, Arizona with his wife, Lisa Frank.

To learn more about the author, visit: **www.ArttFrank.com**

Acknowledgements

There are and have been so many individuals who have supported me in my life and have encouraged me in everything I did, whether it was in music, acting, composing, singing, teaching, playing, and, in the writing of my memoirs. It is a long and beautiful list, and they are…

James and Shirley McClinch, parents of my wife, Lisa, executive producers of my tribute CD, "Looking for the Light: A Tribute to Chet Baker," released on the CCB (Chet & Carol Baker) label.

Karen Pecoraro of North Carolina, my first daughter from a previous marriage.

Earla Porch, my former wife and mother of our three wonderful children, Arthur II, Rhonda Shaw and Kathy Barry.

Carol Baker, Chet's loyal and loving wife and mother of their three wonderful children, Dean, Paul and Melissa (Missy), and Paul's two sons, Chad and Chet, and Missy's daughter, Jasmine.

Chet's first son, Chesney Aftab, from a previous marriage.

Sharon Stone, Academy Award-nominated, iconic film star and friend.

Glenn Berenbeim, Screenwriter and 'king of compression.'

Dave Brubeck - longtime friend and jazz icon, who always encouraged me to 'keep on playing in my own sweet way,' and, Iola, his loving and devoted wife.

Stan Levey - Legendary Be Bop drummer and friend, and his son, Bob Levey.

Charlie 'Yardbird' Parker - Be Bop immortal.

Bob Mover, Jack Pelzer, Hal Galper, Harold Danko, Hod O'Brien, Phil Markowitz, Cameron Brown, Warren Chiasson, Dennis Irwin, Scott Lee, Rich Perry, Dave Liebman and Ali Ryerson.

Phil Bowler - bassist extraordinaire who introduced me to record producer…

Michael Armando - CEO of MJA Records, Inc., who produced and released my first CD as a leader, Waltz for Sharon Stone and my other recorded works, both live concert format and in studio.

Dave Langzatell - Trumpeter/composer.

Tim Schaffner - Publisher/drummer, who published my book on Bop drumming, Essentials For The Be Bop Drummer.

Pete Swan – Jazz drummer and Music editor of my book on Bop drumming.

Matt Criscuolo - Alto player and composer.

Ken Barry - Tenor saxophonist/composer.

Roscoe Freund - Jazz drummer.

Don Doane - Trombone great, who always told me to 'never give up'

Graham Bruce - Bop trumpeter great, & Nik Bariluk - jazz pianist. Both men co-composers of my compositions.

Tony Frank - Jazz trumpeter/singer, who was instrumental in promoting my name and my music all over the globe via his popular Internet jazz radio show from Tucson, AZ.

Jack & Lucille Dolab - Spiritual friends, prayer warriors and fans of both Chet's and my music.

All the great Bop musicians I had the opportunity of 'sitting in' with along storied 52nd Street & Broadway.

All the other great musicians I performed with during the last 60 years of my blessed life.

All my other musician friends and loyal Chet fans throughout the world.

And a special mention to Dr. Stuart Miller, Internist, of Trumbull, Ct. and Dr. Michael Habib, Pulmonologist, V.A. Hospital of Tucson, Az.

May almighty God touch the hearts and minds of every person who reads this book of memoirs; that they may come away with a totally different outlook of the man who has been so misrepresented, misunderstood and maliciously maligned for the better part of his adult musical life. If anyone may see a need or a reason to judge the man, Chet Baker, then let him be judged for the poignantly beautiful, melodic and lyrical music he put forth from his horn and from his singing rather than for his physical weakness - for all of us have weaknesses at one time or another during our lifetimes.

Therefore, as one of the passages from The Book I live by states,

> "*Judge not, that you be not judged. For with what judgment you judge, you shall be judged: and with what measure you mete, it shall be measured to you again.*"
>
> **Matthew 7: 1- 2**

Printed in Great Britain
by Amazon

38821193R00131